the 7
TRUTHS
of
LIFE

Syd,
I am so proud of
the beautiful young lady
you have become! I am so
proud of you —
continue to be the "star" you
are! Love,
Uncle, Senghor 2010

SENGHOR POPE

the 7 TRUTHS of LIFE

YOUR LIFE, YOUR TERMS

TATE PUBLISHING & *Enterprises*

The 7 Truths of Life
Copyright © 2010 by Senghor Pope. All rights reserved.

No part of this publication may be reproduced, stored in a retrieval system or transmitted in any way by any means, electronic, mechanical, photocopy, recording or otherwise without the prior permission of the author except as provided by USA copyright law.

The opinions expressed by the author are not necessarily those of Tate Publishing, LLC.

Published by Tate Publishing & Enterprises, LLC
127 E. Trade Center Terrace | Mustang, Oklahoma 73064 USA
1.888.361.9473 | www.tatepublishing.com

Tate Publishing is committed to excellence in the publishing industry. The company reflects the philosophy established by the founders, based on Psalm 68:11,
"The Lord gave the word and great was the company of those who published it."

Book design copyright © 2010 by Tate Publishing, LLC. All rights reserved.
Cover design by Amber Gulilat
Interior design by Stephanie Woloszyn

Published in the United States of America

ISBN: 978-1-61663-343-1
1. Self-help / Personal Growth / General
2. Self-help / Motivational & Inspirational
10.05.24

Dedication

Firstly, I dedicate this book to my mother, Elaine Stewart Pope. Thank you for allowing me the freedom to explore the possibilities of what I could become versus what others thought I should become.

Secondly, I dedicate this book to my friends and family who have supported me throughout a lifetime of pursuing my desires.

Thirdly, I dedicate this book to all those who have dreamed their dreams and then turned those dreams into their reality.

Lastly, I dedicate this book to my wife and two little girls, who have given me the strength and inspiration that was needed to complete this work. I hope that this book will serve as an instructional manual for you to live the life of your choice, intentionally designed for you by you.

Acknowledgments

I would like to acknowledge all those that have been a part of this process that I refer to as my life. There have been so many people that have played a role in my life that it would be impossible to name everyone. So I will limit the individual acknowledgments in an effort to be brief.

Thanks to all that contributed to the writing, editing, and designing of this book, workbook, lecture series, and coaching platform. Thanks for allowing me the opportunity to bounce ideas off of you and for reading and rereading the many versions of this work. A special thanks to Bobby Steele for keeping me on task and reminding me constantly of my purpose, which was the completion of this work. Another special thanks to my original editor, Elisa Clayton, for believing in the project and contributing so much of your very valued input.

To every friend, family member, or business acquaintance, whether past or present, you have all impacted my life in some shape, form, or fashion. I now realize that we entered one another's life for the purpose of us both experiencing whatever came of our relationship, whether brief or extensive, good or bad. I also thank and appreciate you for coming into my life or allowing me in yours to participate in my becoming the me that I was destined to be. You are too numerous to name, but you know who you are when you read these words; you will know in your heart that I was individually writing this for and saying thank you to *you*.

I would like to thank my surrogate parents who continued the parenting process after the loss of my mother during those critical years of my life. It was your support and direction that helped to guide my steps as I attempted to find my way. My Aunt Pat (Patrice Nance), Mama Turner (Vernell Turner), Mr. Turner (Ronell Turner), and Mama Bright and Mr. Bright (Mr. and Mrs. Gene Bright).

To my dad: I would not have believed that a parent could have that much influence on who a child would become in life if I hadn't seen how much of myself I see in you. I don't know if it's DNA or the long talks that have led me to take on so many of your characteristics. Thanks for giving me the fire needed to continue to push forward when things are there toughest.

To my business partners from birth, my two older brothers, Ronald and Malcolm Pope. You have always been a source of inspiration and the main reason for my staying motivated to do and be more. Over the years, I have often been told that I have had an unfair advantage, a head start, a competitive edge, and a support structure that has blessed me and everything that I do, and my answer is always the same: naw, those are just my brothers. Thanks for the belief and support through the good times and the bad.

My other three daughters, Kai, Sani, and Maia, I look at you as my three little girls. I carefully considered each word that hit these pages because as I wrote them, it was you three that kept my words honest, clear, and driven by the knowledge that one day you may take these words and use them to intentionally design the life that you choose to experience. This is the greatest gift you can give yourself, and so this is my greatest gift to give you. I wrote this book for you and your two sisters; Uncle Senghor loves you!

Last but not least, to my wife, Claribel, thank you for allowing me to experience how it feels to be in a lifelong relationship with a best friend and the love of my life at the same time. Thanks for allowing me to chase my dreams and fulfill my purpose. I can only hope that one day I can return to you what you have given to me. I also must thank you for giving me my two inspirations and my reasons why—my children, Elaina and Leia Pope. By fulfilling my destiny, I arm you with the belief that all things are possible and that you can become anything you choose to. I also thank you for teaching me that without fear, love can't exist and what it means to love without conditions. Elaina, my countless dreams of you coming true is what makes me know that there is order in this universe and that there are no accidents. Leia, you confirmed everything that I have always known, for you are an exact duplicate of the two sides of who I am, and you are my mini me.

Table of Contents

Introduction

My life has always been, and continues to be, a predetermined series of events designed to prepare for and catapult me toward my destiny. This is not a unique scenario occurring only in my life. Life is designed this way for all of us. It turns out that this is a part of the self-supporting design of the universe.

What if you could look into the future and see all of life's possibilities for yourself and were afforded the opportunity to choose one? What if you then were given the chance to go back and preshape the events, the people, and the situations that would bring about the perfect plan to accomplish the life you envisioned for yourself? In this scenario, there are only two rules. The first rule is the people involved in your life are able to choose whether they desire to play out their roles in your masterpiece. You can give hints, influence them, and even utilize all types of synchronistic events, situations, reminders, and people to point them in the direction that fulfills your grand design. The second rule is before returning back to live out this perfectly designed plan for your life, you have to forget that you ever designed a plan. Therefore, in addition to all of the hints that you have setup for your friends and other people involved in your masterpiece, you must create a second set for yourself. With this predesigned course in place, do you think you would have a good shot at living the life of your choosing? Bear in mind although all of the thousands of pieces to your puzzle will seem unrelated, you are born with a deeper inner knowing that in the end all of the pieces of the puzzle will fit together perfectly and create the vision you imagined, prayed for, and have seen in your dreams.

This is how the universe has worked in my life, and as you recount the events and people in your life, you will realize that the universe has worked this way in yours. You may have heard it said that there are no accidents in the universe. Everything that happens to you has a reason and is a part of your purpose, for we're all born with our unique missions embedded in our souls. Some of us have peeled away enough layers of ourselves to discover what that unique mission is and many have actually lived it.

Finding Your Purpose

The question is often asked, "How does one discover one's purpose?" This is a complicated question, and the answer is equally elusive as the question. As a matter of fact, the answer varies from person to person and is just as individualized as the person that is asking. Some people find their purpose and other people's purpose finds them. If you examine the events of your life, you will see this process unfold just as if you had completed the previously described exercise. Upon reflection, you will discover a series of seemingly unrelated events that when viewed from a distance fit together perfectly to attract the people, places, and events that shape your life into the exact manifestation that it currently represents. When I'm asked this question, I try to provide people with some general answers (hints, if you will) that point them in the direction that leads to their own self-discovery of this answer.

Generally, your unique mission can be found in your inner deepest desires. Whether it's the most basic of desires, like survival, food, love, and companionship or even complex desires such as fulfillment and enlightenment, all living things have desires. It is these desires that fuel all of creation. Regardless of whether you believe in the big bang theory or evolution, both of these have desire as their motivating factors.

Now, some will argue a strong case for not desiring anything, but even the desire not to desire something is still a desire within itself.

Every change that happens, whether it's a slow one like evolution or a drastic one manifested out of thin air, desire is always the underlying catalyst. Discover what you desire the most to do, be, or have, and this will generally land you pretty close to the answer of what your soul's purpose is. You may even find that on your way to achieving your desire that it is merely a stepping-stone to an awakening that will eventually lead you to your ultimate purpose in life. This book is designed to help you discover your purpose and live it.

How This Book and You Met

This book is part of your desire manifesting. This is where your desire to find and live your purpose has intertwined with my desire to bring forth a book designed to help you not only discover your purpose but to manifest it through your intentions to have it. This book, like all the people, situations, and things that come in and out of your life, is a tool for the fulfillment of your purpose. Just for a second, think about how you happened upon this book. Did a friend recommend it? Did you see it on a bookshelf somewhere and felt an urge to get it? Or perhaps you came in contact with this book in a more overt way. As you ponder the answer, keep in mind that no matter how this book ended up in your hands, everything happens for a reason, and there are no accidents. You discovered this book just at the right time to receive the information that you are seeking right now. This book is the next step in your evolutionary process, or as it was for me and many others, it could be your big bang. In either case, this book, like everything that you encounter, is a part of the process of your discovering the you that your soul desires to be.

How to Approach This Information:

I believe that there are many different levels of truth and that my truth is just that: my truth. This doesn't mean that my truth has to be your truth or your truth has to be mine. Nor does it mean that my truth is right and yours is wrong, or vice versa. It's the places where our truths are aligned that we have the opportunity to exist as one. It is when our truths diverge that we have the opportunity for further self-discovery and the chance to discover a new truth, a clearer way, and even higher truths. If we all remain stuck thinking or believing alike, then there will never be any advancement in the spiritual world or the physical. This is where most of the people who are in conflict with organized religion base their complaint. This is also where the people in the church base their conflicts with those who operate outside of their religious beliefs. As you can clearly see, they both must exist in order for growth to occur in either place. It's the unity of a collection of truths that originally formed organized religion and the church as a body in the first place. The many denominations and manners of worshipping are the offspring of that collection developing into a new truth. This is the manner in which all religions emerged. So if you look close enough, you will see that each school of thought must exist in order for the other to exist. And the same is true for us as individuals. So, as you approach this information, try to remember that it is your current collection of truths that brought you here to confirm, expand, or develop new truths. As you read along, some of the concepts in this book may challenge a few of your current beliefs. Remember that this is where our truths diverge, and as some of them confirm things that you have already known, know that this is where we embrace our oneness. It's the gray areas that offer us the chance to expand our current set of beliefs and allow us to stretch into newer and grander dimensions of ourselves. As you explore the pages of this book, you will find that there are some truths that are the truth, irrespective of our beliefs about them. It is these truths that I believe that the *Seven Truths of Life* represents. I've heard it said that "the truth just is and it can neither be proven nor denied but you always recognize it when you are in its presence."

THE 7 TRUTHS OF LIFE

The Purpose of the 7 Truths of Life

Each of the seven truths is an individual part of the process of creation. They are not secrets, and they don't have to be discovered or taught to you. As a matter of fact, all seven of them have not only been known by all people throughout the ages, they're already known by you. You were born with this process imbedded in your soul, for you are part of this process. Your reading this book is just a chance for your higher self to help your lower self remember (re-member: to put back together) that which it already knows.

What I love most about these seven truths is that they are not truths that are far-fetched or hard to understand; most are things that many of you will already be familiar with and have heard said many times over in many different ways but probably never in this way. Ideally, if life is a process of creation and each of these seven truths makes creation possible, then the purpose of this book is to reacquaint you with the seven truths of life and remind you how to apply them.

How This Book Will Impact You

This book and the seven truths described in it are designed to help you identify your purpose and manifest it. You will learn how these same truths have shaped the lives of everyone who's ever walked this planet. Each truth and its accompanying description will allow you to lay the groundwork for discovering and creating the circumstances of your most desired life. The seven truths will also be described in their highest forms for utilization in the design of a life plan that manifests the life you choose for yourself. This is where the accompanying workbook or your personal journal will come into play. Your responses to the questions raised by each of these seven truths will create the road map toward the fulfillment of your life's purpose. As you learn the highest application of each truth, you are encouraged to write down your personalized responses so that your life plan can begin to emerge. Your life plan will develop into a daily regimen of activities that will put you on purpose and catapult you toward the life that you have predesigned for yourself through this process.

How to Best Apply the Truths Contained Within These Pages

Lastly, as you utilize these truths to manifest the ideal life for yourself, remember that sharing what you've discovered here with others is the quickest way to help others achieve their lives' purpose and realize your own. It's been said that once taught is twice learned or simply that which you do to or for someone else you do to or for yourself. So as you rediscover your truths through these pages, help others rediscover theirs by exposing them to what you've learned and complete the circle.

The Process of Creation Defined

The adjective for life is change, and all change is fueled by desire. Desire is the currency and catalyst for all that happens. Since change is constant, everything that's alive is always changing from its birth to its never-ending transformation that we call death. Desire is the motivating factor that propels life forward. Anyone who tells you that it's holy not to desire anything is telling you to work against yourself and the natural laws of the universe. When you desire something, you are basically telling the universe that you would like to change what is into what you desire it to be. This book is designed to teach you how to apply this creative force toward the accomplishment of any and everything that you seek.

The Process of Manifestation

The verb for turning thoughts into things is *to manifest.* It comes from the world of imagination and the Middle English word *manifestus,* meaning visible, and the Latin word *manus,* meaning hand.[1] When you manifest something, you metaphorically reach your hand through the invisible curtain separating the tangible world from the intangible and pull your desired object into existence.[2]

The application of these two processes, creation and manifestation, are what's being taught here as you discover and intentionally live your life's purpose.

The Hero in You

Why, in the movies, does the hero always complete his mission and survive insurmountable odds while those around him fail and are somehow only pawns in the hero's victory? A great example of this is Tom Cruise's movie *The Last Samurai.*

He plays a young man, a soldier from America, who finds himself in Japan, a foreign land, expected to fight and conquer the local enemies of the emperor, the samurai. His job is to train the emperor's army to destroy all those who oppose the emperor and his plans to Westernize his country. After the first battle, our hero, Tom Cruise, finds himself captured by the group he was sent to destroy. His captives spare his life to learn more about him. In turn, our hero learns the ways of the samurai and decides to join them. Eventually, he chooses to fight against the emperor and the army that he was sent to train and lead.

Now, after hundreds and possibly thousands of years of the samurai's existence, the emperor is intent upon destroying and killing them all. After a brutal scene on the battlefield, with the samurai fighting using only bows, arrows, and swords against thousands of trained soldiers with heavy military artillery and guns, all of the samurai are killed, leaving only one person alive out of thousands.

As you probably have figured out by now, it's our hero, Tom Cruise. He is the last samurai, despite the fact that he had just become one a few months earlier. [3]

After watching this film, I, like most of you, rationalize that it's only a movie, and we all know that nothing like this ever happens in real life. That's why we watch movies in the first place. It's a chance for us to suspend our disbelief for 120 minutes and allow ourselves to believe that anything is possible even against the most unrealistic odds. Once that small window of time elapses, we leave the movie theater pumped up, still feeling the residuals of the powerful feeling of being able to accomplish anything, at least for the next thirty or forty minutes. Then reality kicks in, and we say to ourselves, "That was a good movie, but it was just a movie." Yet what if I told you that events like these are happening every day in life? Perhaps in a little less dramatic fashion; nevertheless, they still happen to those whose intentions are fueled by their belief in what they are trying to accomplish regardless of the odds.

For instance, how many times did we witness Michael Jordan get the ball with the entire opposing team knowing in advance that his team would attempt to pass him the ball for the last game-winning shot? The opposing team knew they would need to prevent this in order to win the game. They would even practice multiple scenarios and recruit special defensive players to defend against this exact strategy. The defending team, coaches, fans, and everyone else on planet Earth knew what was about to happen, and Michael still somehow got the ball, made the game winning shot, or led a remarkable comeback. When you examine both film and real-life scenarios like these, they seem like impossibilities. But these incredible displays of the actualizing of one's will have happened many times in the lives of different people.

After all, when you observe the lives of most of the people we idolize, their stories are similar to our film and storybook heroes. They too overcome insurmountable odds and unbelievable situations, just like our movie heroes. Actually, some of their stories, if condensed into a two-hour film script, seem even more improbable than the most unrealistic movies.

Think about the people who've had a significant impact on our world. Whether they're from our past, like Jesus Christ, Benjamin Franklin, and Gandhi, or more recent history, like Michael Jordan, J.F.K, Oprah Winfrey, Dr. Martin Luther King Jr., and Nelson Mandela, their stories are just as remarkable. Their lives condensed into two hours would appear on screen, in many ways, equally as fantastical as our movie heroes.

It's the same in your life as it is in the movies, the only difference being that the film version is a 120-minute highlight of a lifespan of many years, even decades. More importantly, perhaps the main difference between your movie and those famous people previously named is that they have all mastered one or more of the seven truths contained in this book. They have become the conscious creator, director, and star of their lives, and thus they consciously dictate the desired outcome for their lives whereas most people live their lives, at best, as just the unconscious actor. You see, the unconscious actor is not aware that he can create the script and direct the scenes. He just shows up every day to act his part, blindly taking direction from his unconscious thoughts and unconscious reactions to the circumstances of his life as if they were predesigned by someone else. Thus the unconscious actor feels he has no control over the outcome. The principles in this book are designed to teach you how to become the conscious creator, the director, and the star in the number one, blockbuster hit movie, your life, so that you can choose if your character lives happily ever after or dies a slow, miserable death, tormented by failure after failure. Just like the hero in the movie, we are all faced with choices in our lives that either help define who we are or cause us to become something that we never knew we had the ability to become. These challenging, insurmountable, and even life-threatening events are often the very opportunities that we need to discover who we truly are and thus discover our greatness. Whether it's the hero in a two-hour movie or one of our real-life heroes like

Benjamin Franklin, their successes can be attributed to the conscious application of the seven truths discussed in this book.

As before mentioned, these seven truths are not secrets, and they don't have to be discovered or taught. I would venture to say that the seven truths contained in this book have already been said to you, or you have heard them somewhere before in some form or fashion. Most of our highest truths have been repeated so often by so many people in so many different ways that you may regard them as clichés. This is where I feel most of our highest truths are hidden, merely as things people say that have no known foundation of truth and are thus discounted and written off. If these clichés had no merit they would not have been spoken of in every way, in every language, by almost everyone since the beginning of time. The difference that you will find here in this book versus the multitude of times you may have heard them used elsewhere is that here you will learn how these principles shape the life that you currently live and how you can use these truths to directly impact any aspect of your life that you desire to improve or totally change.

In the past, I used these seven truths from time to time, sometimes consciously but mostly unconsciously, not knowing that I had orchestrated my universe and designed my life. My life was full of ups and downs; one minute I felt that I was on top of the world, and other times I wondered if I was even a part of this world. As I reflected on all the major events in my life, a pattern began to emerge. This analyzing allowed me to realize that every event that I felt was happening to me was actually happening because of me. As I further thought and meditated on this, I realized that these events where being attracted to me by me for the sole purpose of becoming the me that I am today and will be in the future.

If you also review the events that have shaped your life, it will be easy for you to see that each event is connected and represents the unfolding of your life. Once you stop and look closely enough, you will notice that the situations play out into a perfectly designed, well-orchestrated set of events that have been put in place to allow you to attract the current set of experiences that you are now living.

I believe that your life as you currently view it today in its present condition is the total sum of all of the thoughts you have had, the words you have spoken, and the actions you have taken. As a matter of fact, what else could it be? All of the events in your life, both major and minor, are things that were created by you versus things that happened to you. Whether you see them as good luck, bad luck, karma, synchronicity, or a blessing, if you sit and reflect back on all of the memorable events that have happened in your life in their entirety, you can easily see that these events were not accidents that lead you to where you are today. As you recount the events, you will begin to see the perfection in this well-choreographed and thoroughly developed series of events that have formed your life and brought about your current set of circumstances. With even the slightest retrospect, you will recognize that no computer program or group of people could have generated events so perfectly executed to unfold into your current life. This is what I call God's plan unfolding in your life. For some people, like me, it has taken years of self-discovery, outside coaching, and many hours of reflecting to discover their soul's purpose or life's mission. For others, it happened in the blink of an eye, through a major event. And some people have known their purpose from birth. These people are said to be born to do a certain thing.

Occasionally, I hear people say that they've been doing what they are successful at since the ages of two and three years old. Now, I can't even remember what I was doing at that age, but these people we often say were born to do what they do, and they very often become our heroes. I would venture to say that we are all born knowing our mission; it's just that those who decide not to let other people, circumstances, and other things turn them away from it; and stay the course of what they know to be true for them get the chance to experience having it the fastest. These people have mastered the first truth to obtaining whatever it is they desire.

I remember hearing a story about Oprah Winfrey when she was a little girl around five or six years old. She was sitting on the back porch as her grandmother washed clothes by hand and was hanging them out to dry. As her grandmother wrung water out of the clothes, she chastised young Oprah and told her that she should stop playing and pay attention and learn how to tend to the clothes the same way because one day she too would have to do the same thing. And I will never forget the narrator of this story commenting about young Oprah thinking to herself, *No, Grandma, I will never have to do that as a way of life for myself.* The narrator said that this thought was coming from the mind of a young girl who knew nothing but poverty.[4]

So here she was, surrounded by images that were the opposite of what she held in her head for herself, and through this she was able to see the life that she knew was in her future. You see, what Oprah and those like her have in common is they have mastered the first truth.

The First Step to Getting What You Desire From Life is:
You Must First Identify and Become Crystal Clear About What it is That You Truly Want.

For those of us that wait years to discover this or take years to act on it, the process always begins with becoming clear about what you want. For some of us, we have found out what we wanted by identifying the things that we didn't want through a process of elimination. This is the long way, but it is the way that most often we choose to discover our life's purpose. However we choose to get there, it's only when we become clear about what we desire that we can begin to see God's plan unfolding in our lives, catapulting us toward achieving it.

I read a book called *The Power of the Subconscious Mind* by Dr. Joseph Murphy. In this book, the author suggested that you ask your subconscious mind as you go to sleep at night to wake you up at an exact time the following morning.[5] I tried it, and it worked. That small experiment reminded me that I had done this many times in the past but in different ways and had gotten the same or similar results. One instance stands out more than any other. I was particularly troubled by a reoccurring dilemma that I often found myself faced with. My dilemma was how do I do what I love and make enough money to provide for my family while doing it? This often troubled me because I prided myself on always following my passion and only doing things that brought me fulfillment, which was easy to do in my younger years. However, as I got older, got married, and started a family, what seemed to come so naturally was no longer enough to consistently pay the bills. This is what often happens to our dreams; we put them on the shelf and do what's responsible. Nonetheless, I was faced with a familiar decision to make: do I stay in the business that I enjoy, or do I change directions and do something less fulfilling for me but more accommodating for those affected by my choices? I knew from my newfound ability that I could respond with the knowledge that the answer could be found in the question. So I asked myself the question, "How can I make more money doing what I enjoy, which was investing in real estate, but do it with less time committed?" I asked myself this question repeatedly as I contemplated how to remain in this industry that I loved and still accomplish my goals of more income with less input on my part, both in time and effort. As the second day of this continued thought passed, I started to wonder if I should look into other industries to find the answer or if I should even consider taking on a different aspect of this industry that could possibly help me accomplish what I was after. As I finished my workday and began to retire for the evening, I sat there in my home office staring at the wall, contemplating this question more and more. It was at that point when I thought to myself, *The answer must lie in the question.* Invigorated, I immediately got up and wrote the question on the whiteboard in my office. I then sat again and stared at the question. With this question burning brightly in my mind, I went to bed and fell asleep without giving it very much more thought. At about four o'clock in the morning, I woke up to a loud voice that I somehow knew was in my head and not somewhere in my house. As I cleared from the grogginess and tried to think about what the loud voice in my head was saying to me, I heard the voice simply and plainly say, "Do bigger deals." I sat up on the corner of my bed and said to myself, "What in the world does that mean, 'do bigger deals'?" Rather than sit there trying to figure it out, I immediately got up and headed to my home office, grabbed a pen and paper, and wrote down what I heard. As I sat there contemplating what this loud voice was trying to tell me, I looked up at my whiteboard and saw the question that at the time I had forgotten that I had written down before going to bed. The question was, "How can I make more money in the real estate industry with less time and effort committed?" I looked down at the paper at what I had scribbled, and there was the answer as simple and as plain as day: "Do bigger deals." I don't know how something so simple could have escaped me. Why an answer this easy to interpret did not come to me days earlier or why it came to me in the middle of the night bewilders me. It was then I remembered Dr. Joseph Murphy's book and asking my subconscious to wake me up at 4:27 a.m. From this time on, when faced with a burning question or dilemma, I responded with my newly found ability. This hit me like a ton of bricks, the fact that God had set the universe up in a way that would allow us to ask the questions that would lead to the answers we needed to live successful and fulfilled lives.

As far back as I can remember; I have always had a desire to serve others. From being a little kid wanting to make breakfast for my older siblings, to founding companies for the sole purpose of the enrichment of others, to this book, its accompanying workbook, and lecture series, I have always found myself wanting to help others fulfill their dreams. I don't know where this desire came from, considering I didn't grow up with an overabundance of anything material, so I can only assume that it must be part of my purpose for being here. This knowledge of my purpose didn't come as a flash of instant insight like it does for some; it sort of evolved over time through a series of wonderful and sometimes very weird events.

This book is a recounting of many of those events that shaped my life and helped me to learn my purpose. This book and the outline of the seven truths are simply answers to questions asked. I had an idea before I began to write this book of what I wanted the subject matter to be about and the purpose for which I hoped the book would serve. However, I had no idea of the format or even that there would be such a thing as seven truths of anything. As a matter of fact, the one thing I felt that the literary world did not need was another seven steps to something. As I struggled to formulate how to communicate a simple, logical approach toward creating one's life as one would like for it to be designed, I realized that this book is the manifestation of the collective consciousness of many people. So I meditated on how to write about my experiences in a way that would bring about a defined way to intentionally manifest one's desires versus the random, synchronistic manifestations that appeared in my life that I later recognized as my own creation. As I meditated and thought about how to format and tell this story in a way that people could follow and benefit from, I realized that this feat was a much larger undertaking than I had originally thought. It was at that moment that I remembered that all I had to do was ask the universe to define this work for me rather than laboring for months and potentially years just to figure out what I was going to write. All I had to do was make myself available to receive what had already been predestined for me but not predetermined and that it was my availability, not my ability that was keeping me from realizing my ultimate goals. I already had identified that the problem with people like me who think they can do it all is that they often try to. This was a major obstacle for me. I had a tendency to become preoccupied with all of my many potential accomplishments and never made myself available for the things that I was put here to do. Subsequently, it was easy for me to diagnose this problem in myself and recognize what was being said to me when a friend told me that if I could just sit still long enough that I would become what we both knew I was supposed to become. I thought to myself, *If it's really that simple—just ask the question, make myself available to receive the answer, and let the universe do the rest—then even I could do this.* So in an effort to begin responding with my new ability, that night, I asked myself the question over and over again: "What is the subject matter of this book and how should this book be formatted to benefit those who come to it?" I went to sleep that night with the expectation that when I awoke the next morning, or sometime throughout the course of the night, the outline would come to me, and I would know exactly the format and how to write this book. I awoke the next morning surprised that there was no dream, no loud voice, nothing. As I thought about it again, that next day I wondered if I was supposed to figure it out myself or if all I truly had to do was ask like I had done so many times before. So for the next few nights, I meditated and asked myself the same question again and again. I even slept with a pen and notebook next to the bed, expecting my answer to come through and still nothing happened. Several days passed and I found out that I had to leave for an unexpected business trip to Florida, which threw me out of my routine. After working all day in Florida, I retired that night to bed exhausted without doing my nightly question asking and meditating. I fell asleep at about midnight, and just as I heard myself go into one of those deep sleeps (meaning I can hear myself snoring) I heard a loud voice say, "First you must become clear about what it is that you want." As I lay there wondering whether I was dreaming or not, I remember saying to myself, "What?" I sat up in my hotel bed and thought to myself, *What do I want?* I wondered what that meant, and then I remembered the question I had been asking for the previous four or five days. I instantly knew that the universe had begun writing this book. Every night after that first night, like clockwork, I was awakened at about 3:30 a.m. with the same loud voice with truths one through seven, only skipping one or two nights in between. Religiously, every night I got up and wrote down what I heard and whatever brief explanation that sometimes accompanied each truth that didn't make sense just as a statement. Here is what came out:

1. The first thing that you must do to get anything that you want is you must become clear about what it is that you want. Decide what you want and become clear about it. Decide it and choose nothing else.

2. Do your beliefs and your attitude support you getting what you want? Do you believe that you can have it and what are your attitudes about it?

3. What is your game plan for getting what you want? Are your goals in support of what you want?

4. Think. Think thoughts in support of what you want. Visualize your highest thoughts about it and view it with your strongest feelings. Think about what you want and nothing else and never about what you don't want. Use imagery and feelings to think. Visualization is the highest form of thinking.

5. Speak. Speak only words that are in support of what you want. Affirmations and incantations: speak your truest words about it using the greatest commanding words ever spoken: I AM. Words are thought expressed.

6. Actions. Take the highest actions in support of it. The greatest action you can take is to cause someone else to experience in his or her life that which you wish to experience in yours.

7. Thankfulness. You must be thankful in advance for that which has not happened yet. Proper prayer is your ability to pray and meditate on the things that are possible for your life and having enough faith to allow God and yourself to bring them about.

As awesome and intriguing as the idea of these seven truths having the capability to work in the lives of those willing to design their life plans by implementing these truths was, I still found myself questioning many aspects of it. I knew that each truth worked and could work independently of the other truths because I had seen remarkable things happen in my life due to the mastery of just one or two truths whether used in combination or not. The thing that troubled me was the doubt that I had that I was the right person to bring forth this message. Had I truly lived a life created and directed by me, or had I been the product of circumstance? Would the fact that my life took so many ups and downs, good turns and bad, take away from the message? Would people miss the message because they focused on judging the messenger versus the message? As I thought about it, I realized that it was for these very reasons that I was bringing this message forth. The fact that I had been through a lot is what qualified me to have a story to tell in the first place. Someone once said, "You cannot have a testimony without a test." Even bearing all of that in mind, I still had to be totally certain that if others consciously used these *seven truths*, they could literally manifest anything they chose in their life, especially since that is what's being promised by the message of this book. Therefore, I decided to test the truths in a way that would prove their validity to me, a few friends, and family members.

The Test

To test this process, I decided to make some bold predictions of what the desired outcome would be if I became totally aligned with what I believed was the formula for manifesting the things that I wanted in my life. To test this theory, I decided to make these bold claims of what I would manifest via these seven truths to some of the most critical people of me that I knew: my immediate family. It's not that my family wasn't supportive of me; it's just that they had heard me say that I was going to do a lot of things. As I began the process of identifying what I wanted and deciding when I wanted these things to show up in my life, I realized that I would have to set the standards for what I was going to accomplish vastly out of my control, so much so that no one could deny that what I had accomplished came through something much bigger than myself. There would be no way that I could have accomplished this on my own. So I announced to my wife, brothers, and a few close friends one night at dinner what I had been working on and what I was planning to accomplish. I explained to them how the seven truths came to me in a series of dreams and that I would work this plan to create a million dollars in net worth by my thirty-fourth birthday. At that time,

I had about 150,000 dollars in cash and assets. As I had imagined, I received the usual laughs and comments like, "Okay, Senghor, here we go again" or "Yeah right, Senghor. How do you propose to do that, considering your birthday is a little more than sixty days away?" Most of the laughs, criticisms, and mocking disbelief that I received was attributed to how I planned to accomplish this feat because I had made crazy predictions before and accomplished them. Once I calmed their laughter down, I told them the rest of the plan. I explained to them that not only would I do this by my birthday, but I would prove that just following these truths alone was all that you needed to do because the universe would do the rest. I would accomplish this goal, and I would not do any work whatsoever to make this happen. Because of the nature of the business I was in, it was not far-fetched to find a few great real estate deals, get them under your control, and generate a million dollars in a short amount of time (maybe not in sixty days, but still in a short amount of time). I explained that I would do nothing other than focus on what I wanted, work my daily regimen of the seven truths, and everything else would just appear. This made everyone stop and say, "Okay, now this I've got to see."

That night, I thought to myself, *Boy this is a bold plan, and I better start working these seven truths right away.* About ten minutes into my meditation, I realized that I couldn't get rid of the thought that this prediction may have been a little bit more than what I should have tried to take on. Plus, the second that it doesn't work, no one will take my book or the seven truths seriously again. So I decided that night to change the number from one million to 350,000. This I felt was doable, considering the time frames, and it still would be a major accomplishment, considering the fact that I planned to do nothing other than work the plan I had designed for myself through the seven truths. I quickly recanted my bold prediction to everyone that was at the dinner the previous night and told them of the new prediction, which they admitted would still be major if it happened. Several weeks passed before I went back to work my plan, probably due to the lack of enthusiasm for my smaller goal. However, I still knew I could manifest the 350K just by following the truths and nothing else. As I sat down to rewrite truth number three, the goal, I scratched through the one million dollars and changed it to 350,000. As I wrote the numbers 350,000, I thought to myself, *Why am I setting limits on what God can do through the most powerful tool that's ever been created, the universe?* And the fact that I knew through all of my life's experiences that each of these steps had helped me create miracles in my life independent of one another and that if I used them together, surely this could happen. In that instant, I adopted my original plan and began to work it. I then called everyone back and told them that the original prediction was back on. The very first person I called brought me to a very sobering realization that my birthday was now thirty-three days away, and at this point nothing had happened! Even with that in mind, I made the rest of my calls and rewrote my entire plan and this was it:

- What do I want: Being worth a million dollars in net worth by my thirty-fourth birthday with little to no effort on my part.

- What are my beliefs and attitudes about what I want: I believe that these seven truths have individually created miracles in my life, and used together, I would manifest this goal.

- My goal: To work the seven truths of life plan twice a day until I reached my goal of one million dollars in net worth by my thirty-fourth birthday.

- Thought: Visualize a picture of myself on the cover of a magazine with the caption reading "Self-made Millionaire" with the issue date being my birthday.

- Word: I am thirty-four years old, and I am a millionaire!

- Action: I will mentor one person a day to help him or her toward the achievement of his or her financial goals.

- Thankfulness: I am thankful in advance for that for which I am aligning myself with. So I will act as if what I want has already happened.

Over the next few days, a series of seemingly unrelated things started to happen that I didn't realize at the time was part of my manifesting what I wanted. The first thing was a young lady called me up that I had not talked to in a while who was a real estate agent in Jacksonville, Florida. Several months prior, I had submitted an offer to purchase a house through her. She asked me if I was still interested in the house. Almost a year had passed since I had it under contract. I told her if it became available I would still be interested. She then explained that all of the title issues were cleared and that the sellers remembered I had wanted to buy the property. If I still was interested, they would entertain a lower amount than I had originally contracted for. Now, any logical thinking person would have thought at the time, *Wow this is starting to work,* but for some reason, I didn't equate this event to my plan. So I placed the property under contract and potentially increased my net worth by 100K. A few days later, a friend of mine called and asked if I still had some investment properties in Florida that I was looking to sell. He had just freed up some money and wanted to invest in real estate. I told him I did and that I would e-mail him the different properties that I was thinking of selling. Later that day, he called me back and told me that he had found one that he wanted to buy. I was hesitant because this property had a major upside, and I wanted to hold it while the rest of the street was developed. However, I didn't want to rent it and maintain it while the development happened. My friend explained to me what he wanted to do, which worked out perfectly. His plan would allow me to participate in the upside when the house sold, and at the same time I would not have to rent it out and deal with tenants while the rest of the street caught up to the newly revitalized portion of the neighborhood. This deal allowed me to make forty thousand dollars up front and maintain an equity position of forty thousand dollars. It also helped me realize the 50K I had already taken out of the deal. By this time, I should have said to myself, "This is really happening," but I didn't see it unfolding. Since I wasn't working for these deals and they were just coming to me, or because I was still so far away from a million dollars, I didn't even start to keep a tab. As I went to bed that night, I did my visualization, my affirmations, and glanced at the calendar. There were only thirteen days left.

The next day, I ran around doing a few last-minute things before leaving town. I had to take a trip to the west coast for business. Whenever I'm on that side of the country, I try to squeeze all of my visiting of friends and family in for obvious reasons. I planned to be gone about seven days and be home in time for my birthday. As usual, the second I got on the road, I lost all bearings on my daily regimen. I looked up and four or five days had passed since I had last worked my seven truths life plan. My birthday was only seven or eight days away, and I knew that nothing short of a miracle would have to happen. As I sat there getting ready to start my meditation, it hit me. I had already made great strides toward hitting my goals. The house that I had gotten under contract and closed had just come to me. The deal that my friend had proposed was just perfect, and it too got me closer to my goal. I felt a rush of excitement come over me as I asked myself, "What's next?" and "Why didn't I realize that it was working sooner? Did I miss any opportunities while I was unconscious of what was happening?" As I worked my plan that morning, I could not help but expect the very next call to be some-thing miraculous. Whatever happened next had to be big because I figured at that point I had about 400K under my control, provided everything went as planned.

Later that day, I got a call from an investor friend of mine. We talked about the different deals we had on the table and just got caught up. As we concluded the conversation, he mentioned he had a deal that had passed by his desk. He knew it was outside of my normal investing preference, but he thought he would just run it by me anyway. I just knew that this was the deal to put me over the top, but as he talked about the deal, the numbers didn't work for me. The young lady who had the house under contract was selling the house for 800K, and the house was worth 1.2 million. Not only was this deal a lot more than I was comfortable pursuing, as an investment property, it still would have left me about 200K short. So I told my friend I wasn't interested; however, he insisted that I at least go out and look at the house. I explained to him that I was on the west coast and wouldn't be returning for a few days. He insisted that I send someone by to at least take pictures and e-mail them to me. A few months prior, I had described to him the house I wanted to find to live in, and he felt this house was perfect. Mainly out of curiosity, I sent someone out to take pictures and e-mail them to me. The instant the e-mail opened, I knew this house was going to work out.

I immediately called my friend and told him I wanted to negotiate with the seller of this property to see if I could lower the price and prepared a written offer. He explained to me that he had already been on the phone with the person we thought was the seller and found that she was not the owner of the property. The property was a bank-owned foreclosure, and she had lost the contract. He told me that she was requesting an extension on the contract and recommended that I submit an offer directly to the bank as a backup. Now, I was very familiar with this process. I did this between ten and twenty times a month just to get one to two deals accepted, and it still normally took a week or two to get a fully effectuated contract from the bank. At that rate, it would take me a month or two past my birthday deadline even if somehow the young lady's deal fell through and my offer was accepted. What happened next was nothing short of the miracle I was expecting. The next day, the bank denied the other buyer's request for an extension on her already sixty-day overdue contract. The bank representative then called my friend and confirmed that they had received my offer. They planned to review it and respond in writing over the next week or two. The offer I submitted was substantially lower than the original price that the young lady had offered to sell it to me. It was so much lower that if accepted, the amount would have put me over the top of the monetary portion of the goal but would miss the time allotted.

By the time I was home in Atlanta, I was no longer focused on my goal of a million dollars before my thirty-fourth birthday, which was now only hours away. My birthday is on January 9, but we always celebrate it on the eighth since my wife's birthday is on the seventh. This has become a tradition of ours; rather than planning two parties, we just do something together on the day in between. As the evening progressed, I could not stop talking or thinking about this house that I had submitted an offer on just a few days prior. Later that evening, I saw that my friend, the investor that originally told me about the deal, had called several times. I assumed he was calling to tell me that he was either running late or that he would not make it at all, which was odd because he never missed a party. As I looked at the caller ID, I noticed that he had called repeatedly, and by this time it was after midnight, so I became concerned and returned his call. The second he picked up the phone, I heard the excitement in his voice. He explained to me that the bank representative had called him, and they had accepted my offer of $505,000.00, and not only had they decided to accept my offer, but they effectuated the contract with no counter stipulations and faxed the signed contract to me. By this time it, was well after midnight, which was officially my thirty-fourth birthday. I immediately went online to check my faxes. As I went through the faxes, I saw one that had come across earlier that day. I clicked on the e-mail, and there was a fully executed sales agreement from the bank. As I printed the contract and did the math, my net worth value was over one million dollars. I walked into the party that was still in progress and made the announcement in front of the same group that I had, just sixty days earlier, announced my plan to manifest this outcome by utilizing the seven truths process.

As I write this today, almost ten months have passed, and all three of the deals closed as planned, and my goal that materialized in literally sixty days had fully manifested.

When these seven truths were completely outlined, it was clear what the purpose and message behind this book was going to be. It was also clear that all the things that had happened in my life had led me to be the appropriate person bringing it forth. Even though I knew deep inside that I had used each of these principles in my life to bring about many of the things that I will discuss in this book, I knew that it was the completion of this book that would teach me to master and use all of the seven truths in the manner described within these pages.

Congratulations in advance for discovering your life, on your terms, intentionally designed for you by you.

Truth #1

The first step to getting what you want is
to identify what it is that you want.

- Application: What do you want? Decide what you want and become clear about it. Decide it and choose nothing else.

- Explanation: This first step in the process of creation is to identify what you want.

- Manifesting Principle: Change your wants into desires and change your desires into a choosing.

If you are passionately obsessed about it, could not survive if forced to live without it, would lose it if you couldn't choose it, and willing to put everything on the line in order to pursue it, then you've found your purpose.

What do you want?

The number one reason most people never get what they want is they don't know what it is that they want. How can you get something when you are unsure about what it is you desire? One thing I know for certain is that people who achieve anything in their personal lives have this one thing in common: they all clearly know what it is they want. As simple as this may sound, you will be amazed to know that nine out of ten people cannot answer this question regarding what it is they really and truly want, not just on the surface but deep down inside. What is it that you truly want for your life?

The indispensable first step to getting the things you want out of life is this: decide what you want.

—Ben Stein[6]

Many will say off the top of their head that they want to become millionaires, but money is rarely what they truly desire. What people are really saying is they want to have the things that a million dollars can bring them. And even more so, they are really after the feeling that most people associate with having the things they want. So there's a lot more to consider about what you desire to have present in your life than just what is on the surface.

The most essential step in mapping out your life plan is to begin with the end in mind and decide upfront what it is that you want. Someone once told me, "If you don't know where you are going, then any road will get you there." In his book *Conversations with God,* Neal Donald Walsch asked God, "Why do I continue to get such a wide variety of results in my life versus what I want to have present in my life?"[7] The answer to that question was he kept changing his mind about what he wanted.[8] He learned that the quickest way to stop getting a variety of results was to decide what it was he wanted and to stop changing his mind about it.[9] This answer really struck home for me because when I looked back at my life, with all of its ups and downs, the times when I was very successful and the times when I couldn't find my way, I now realize that the reason I had experienced so many different results was due to the number of times I had changed my mind about what I wanted. You see, the people who are the clearest about who they are and what they want, always experience being or having what they want the fastest. These are the people who we say were born to do what they do or that what they do is their calling. However, this could actually be said about all of us. It's just that some of us figure this out sooner while others never figure it out.

When your desires are strong enough you will appear to possess superhuman powers to achieve.

—Napoleon Hill [10]

The very thought of what you want brings you closer to it. The clearer you become about your wants by peeling away the layers, the more focused your wants will become, which will then begin to develop into desires. When you desire something, you have exceeded the petty layers of want and have become undeniably clear about what you seek. Desire requires clarity, and is the higher level of want. Want does not and cannot become desire until you are clear about what you seek, and then it will seek you at the same pace. So when you are vaguely clear about what you want, what you want is only vaguely clear about wanting you. When you decide "This is what I want," then what you want decides the same thing about you and begins to come about just a little bit faster. In other words, what you seek seeks you.

When your want increases to intent, the same thing happens; the intent to fulfill that want increases. That is why the first step to aligning yourself with what you want is to know what it is. Everything that exists in the physical has its nonphysical counterpart. The energy of the physical has its equivalent in the nonphysical form. Thus, when you seek something in the physical world, its energy already exists; therefore, if someone else has been able to align his intention to the energy of that thing, then so can you. If the thing you seek doesn't already exist in its physical equivalent, then your thoughts of it have already begun its creation, for every physical thing that exists originated from thought.

This is what happens when you are inspired; you are in spirit.[11] When you are in spirit, you are now in alignment with the things that are nonphysical in your current reality, which then allows you to bring forth the spiritual or the unseen to the physical.[12]

Now, I know there is a strong argument out there that suggests that wanting something only creates more want, which is absolutely correct. However, you must first know what you want before you can choose its higher version. The higher version of want is desire, and desire (especially the red-hot kind) creates on the highest levels. In order to have desire, you must first have complete clarity, which is why want precedes intent and intent precedes desire and desire precedes a burning desire. Once your desire has become crystallized around your clear intentions to create, certain magical things begin to happen that manifest into reality those things that were originally held as simply a thought of what you wanted.

> By believing passionately in something that still does not exist, we create it. The nonexistent is whatever we have not sufficiently desired.
>
> —Nikos Kazantzakis[13]

However, this is only the beginning. Because in order to move into the manifesting aspects of this process, you must take what you have decided that you want and now choose to have it. The manifesting aspect of this truth becomes a little tricky, for after you have learned how to transform your want into something that you are now choosing, you can never want it again if you plan on having it. You see, the problem with wanting something is you can never have what you want, especially if you want it badly enough. Simply because the very thought of want produces more of that, more want. Certainly, this can be confusing in the beginning, so we will explore this further. You must be saying to yourself "If wanting something produces more want, then why is it considered one of the seven truths?" The reason for this is before you can choose something, you must first desire it, and before you can desire it, you have to want it. Want is the lowest vibration on the chain of creation, but this is where it starts.

Knowing what you want is the first step to getting it. As simple as that sounds, most people struggle with this. To know the true desires of your heart is more than half of what is required to create it.

> For where your treasure is, there your heart will be also.
>
> Matthew 6:21[14]

This is the reason you must do what you love and love what you do. Again, it's a lot easier said then done. Once you've gotten over the first major step of deciding what you want, you must then figure out how to turn what you want into what you do. This can be especially challenging for many of the reasons that we have mentioned before, but the main reason is most people don't believe they can do what they love or love what they do. This saying makes it sound like doing what you love and loving what you do is the same thing, but they are not. Doing what you love could mean a change in career, focusing on a particular part of your career, or even chasing a dream of starting your own business. But loving what you do almost always requires a shift in attitude or your beliefs about what you do. This seems like the easier of the two, but is often far more difficult than a change in career or deciding to chase a dream. As tough of a decision as it may be to leave a career behind to pursue something that you are passionate about, changing your attitude and beliefs about going from something that you do to something that you love to do can be much tougher. This is often the choice many people find themselves having to make, not because they sold out or didn't have what it takes to pursue something else. It's just that sometimes when you get down to it, you may find that your acres of diamonds were right in front of you. If you are not familiar with the story of *Acres of Diamonds* by Russell Conwell, I strongly encourage you to read it. The story is about a wealthy man who leaves his home in search of diamonds and eventually loses everything he owns while traveling the world only to later find after his death that someone else discovers the largest diamond bed ever found in this man's backyard.[15] So don't miss your acres of diamonds by looking for something that you may already have.

This is especially true for the full-time moms and dads of the world who may sometimes think that they would rather be back in their full-time careers doing whatever it was they enjoyed or were extremely good at. But upon further reflection, they realize that nothing could be more rewarding than their tasks of shaping and molding their children.

The size of the answer is always determined by the size of the questions.

—Anonymous

45

So how do we figure out what we ultimately want for our lives beyond the superficial answers of more money, respect, and/or success? The process of uncovering this starts with asking yourself some very specific and defining questions that will lead you to the answers you seek. When we begin to look deeper into what it is that we want for our lives, we have to start looking at the clues that were left behind by those who have found the answer to this question and have gone on to become our heroes and heroines. One of the telltale signs to discovering this is derived by asking yourself, "What am I passionate about?" It's been said that you should either do what you love or love what you do. But in order to truly discover your life's mission, you must dig deep to find out the things you are passionate about doing. It is easy to mistake enjoyment for passion. One of the best descriptions I've ever heard that stuck with me since the moment I heard it came from a professional chef explaining what happens to him when he cooks. He said that when he cooks it is as if the entire world has stopped and during that time he experiences no other sensations other than the joy that comes from doing his passion. While cooking, he never experiences any of the ailments that plague him during his normal daily activities; he never gets tired, hungry, or anything else that he usually experiences while doing other things. My wife says she has the same exact experience while shopping! I quickly recognized this as a clever way to suppress my complaining. So now I tell her to follow her passion for shopping just as long as she can find a way to make money doing it. As you can imagine this did not go over very well.

That brings us to the most puzzling part of following your passion: making money while doing what you love. I have recently discovered that the best way to make money and enjoy it is by doing something you love. What good is it to make great money doing something you hate? This is where many people find themselves after years of doing something that doesn't bring them fulfillment. They become so vested in what they're doing that they feel they can't stop because they're in too far. What began as something that you simply just didn't enjoy, turns into resentment, disgust, and finally hate because it failed to bring you fulfillment. These negative feelings can begin to adversely affect every aspect of your life and can even possibly end it. For this reason, this is the most important aspect that must be explored before anything else.

Recently, I saw a CNN special in which the investigative team traveled all over the world to study various people and their cultures in an effort to uncover the key to their longevity. Some of the people interviewed lived to be as much as 130 to 140 years old and were still productive members of their society. Remarkably, these various groups of people lived on opposite ends of the earth and every place in between. There were variations in their diet, activity levels, stress levels, climate, and many other variables that the researchers attempted to find as common attributes between them. At the end of the investigation, they found that the people who lived the longest only had one real thing in common. I watched the entire program to find out if it was exercise, diet, community, environment, etc., but I was astonished by what they discovered, although it made perfect sense. The one common thing that contributed to their long, healthy, and fulfilled lives was that each person's role in his or her community allowed him or her to do only the things he or she loved doing.

> There is no scarcity of opportunity to make a living at what you love to do; there is only scarcity of resolve to make it happen."
>
> —Wayne Dyer[16]

If a person's passion was cleaning, then that was his or her contribution to his or her community. If another person really loved farming, then that was all his community asked of him. This special investigation taught me a very valuable lesson about finding a way to live from your passion. Not only were they living longer, they were healthier, happier, and more fulfilled. Their communities were also healthy and thriving. Disease was almost nonexistent in these cultures and so was any *dis-ease*. Therefore, in order to be clear about what you truly want, you must discover what you are passionate about.

The second question is, what things do people compliment you on the most? Once I realized that there is a very critical link towards the self-discovery of one's passion and this question, I read it repeatedly, and a few answers began to emerge, so I wrote them down. I even enlisted the help of those closest to me and asked them to choose one characteristic about me they felt most complimented me. I also wrote those down and what I found amazed me. I noticed that the answers from the ten or so people that I had asked and the answers that I personally came up with almost all lead to the exact same thing. And as you complete this exercise, you may even discover that there is something brand-new that you never thought of waiting for you to find it. Upon completion of this exercise, I realized that my passion and what people complimented me on the most or thought was my strong suit were the exact same. This caused me to question why I hadn't asked myself these questions sooner or why had others not volunteered this information sooner. I now realize that this is a process of self-discovery, although it isn't uncommon for others to see things in you that you don't see in yourself. Nevertheless, it is up to the individual to ask these questions and seek out the answers.

When I think about the various ventures I've pursued based on what I wanted at the time, it easily illustrates the previous point. I have attempted more business ventures in more industries than most people would ever consider. When I was in my teens, this was not a problem, for I was always clear about what I wanted, mainly due to the fact that my range of experiences was limited, so I didn't have as many options from which to choose. This would later change and become the main reason for my roller-coaster ride of successes and failures. In my early years, unlike most young people, I knew exactly what I wanted, and I knew exactly how to go about getting it. I decided that I wanted to be an entrepreneur because I wanted to own my business and call all the shots. I had some early work experiences to thank for that. When I was eleven and twelve years old I worked during the summers at the local college doing odd jobs like waxing floors and cleaning the bathrooms of the gymnasium. It wasn't the work that bothered me as much as it was the manner in which the boss treated and talked to me. Often using demeaning language and handing off the worst jobs to those of us who he didn't like, my boss quickly taught me that working for someone was not something I would be willing do for the rest of my life. So at the age of thirteen, I decided that I would mow grass, do odd jobs, or anything other than work for someone else. By the time I was sixteen, I had a successful promotions business doing the one thing I was best at, partying. At times, I earned as much money if not more than most of the parents of my classmates.

What you get is not determined by what you want. It's determined by who you are.

—Anonymous

I sometimes think about why I have gotten such varied results over the years and how often I have started and stopped different businesses, and there is an obvious correlation between the two. I now understand that I had no idea what I truly wanted. For example, in my early years, the times when I was clear about what I wanted, I achieved success with relative ease. On the contrary, when I was unsure about what I wanted, my results varied as much as my thoughts. Doesn't it just make sense that if the things you think about are what become reality, then when you think about a bunch of different things at one time, you will get a bunch of different results? So when I decided for once to predetermine what I would get by deciding in advance what I wanted, I had to first answer the question, "What do I want?" I pondered this question for months before I could begin to uncover what my truest and deepest desires were. As I went through this process, I recounted many of the times when I was absolutely certain of my purpose and my reason for being on this planet, and it was those times that I was most successful and fulfilled. As I think back, I can still feel how I felt during those times, and I asked myself, "What would make me feel that way now? And why do I go from doing something that makes me so fulfilled to doing things that do not?" Those thoughts took me in a different direction, and I began to think about all of the things that I had seemingly failed at and how each of those things made me feel. A pattern began to emerge. I began to see that the times that I was totally clear about what I wanted, I found myself feeling great and thus experiencing what most would consider success. The times that I acted on the things that others wanted for me or the times when I followed something before figuring out if it was in line with what I ultimately wanted, I found myself struggling and feeling very drained and unsatisfied. Now, in retrospect, I realize that every venture was in support of what I ultimately wanted. It's just some ventures were right in line with what I now know is a part of my destiny, and some were designed to show me just how far off track I had gotten.

The final question when discerning what you want is, "What could you not live without?" What activity would you just die if you could not do, or put another way, what would you be willing to die for? I would venture to say that whatever your answers are to these questions, they will land you as close to your true purpose as you can possibly be. Often, we find ourselves so busy doing what is important to everyone else that we rarely find the time to figure out what's most important to us. We often confuse doing what's important for those that depend on us as being the responsible choice, but I believe the exact opposite is true. I believe that true responsibility starts when you do what's important for you first and then find ways to serve others with what comes out of that. Many will argue that's being selfish and self-centered, and I will be the first to agree with them. I believe that if you can't learn to serve yourself, then how will you ever learn to serve someone else? I often share with people that you can't give something away that you don't already possess yourself. Now, let me explain these statements in a little more detail. First, imagine doing what you feel is right for someone that you care about but all the while knowing that it is wrong for you. How do you think this scenario will end? Eventually, most people will realize that they're living a lie and resent themselves and those that they were doing it for in the first place. Others will potentially meet with grimmer consequences that could lead to an early death onset by the torment over the failures of a life half-lived. Then there will be those that decide to live their life based on what's important to them, and by doing so, they have the chance to provide for all those who they wished to serve. These are the people that go on to live a truly successful life full of health, wealth, and happiness. But before this can happen, each person must take the time to figure out what's most important to him or her. Answering these questions will guarantee that you will discover the answer to what your purpose is.

What You Seek You Already Are

What you seek you already are. Aligning yourself with what you seek requires that you do the things necessary in order to have what you are after. Deciding to do the things necessary to get what you are choosing to do, be, or have automatically aligns you with the part of you that already is what you seek to become.

Be what nature intended you for and you will succeed.

—Sydney Smith[17]

Someone once said that you either go within or you will go without. You already have inside of you that which you wish to manifest on the outside of you. For this reason, you will often have people ask if you are already that which you desire to become. How many times has someone mistaken you for the very thing that you have often thought you were supposed to be? How many times has someone asked you if you were a dancer or a preacher or something else that you thought about becoming? The more this happens and you take notice of it, the more you will start to see that sometimes other people can see you for what you already truly are and can be, more so than you can see for yourself. My brothers and I often laugh at how frequently people ask me if I'm a pastor. I quickly tell them, "Not by a long shot." But again and again, strangers will stop and ask me, "What do you do? Are you a pastor?"

As you can see, there are as many ways to discover your purpose as there are options on what your purpose could possibly be. As you begin to pay attention, you will see how all roads seem to lead to the same destination.

Becoming What You Want
Versus Getting What You Want

If who you are could get you what you wanted, wouldn't you already have it? If you don't have the things that you seek, then something must change in order for you to align yourself to receive it. You have to change who you are or change what you want. See, the problem that most of us experience is that once we become aware of what we want, we immediately start to try to figure out the shortest route to obtain it. A better way of putting this is that we try to figure out the smallest amount of effort that we will have to apply in order to get what we are after. The difficulty with that is that all change is painful; the more you resist the changes that must be made, the more those changes will continue to show up as challenges or road blocks toward your accomplishing what it is that you are after. The amount of changes that you have to make is a barometer as to how far away you are from obtaining what you want. The fewer changes that are required, the closer you are. You will know this because people will begin to associate you with what you seek. People will ask, "Are you a certain thing" or "Have you ever thought about becoming a certain thing?" Some will even go as far as telling you that they think you would be great at a particular thing and possibly suggest that you give it a try. Rather than being offended by this, you should start to look at what is being said to you and check the similarities between it and the answers to the questions raised earlier in this chapter.

The mind of man plans his way, but the Lord directs his steps.

Proverbs 16:9[18]

The Prophetess

This very thing began happening to me, and I started to take notice. But it wasn't until someone made me see in myself what they saw in me that I took action, and this book is the result of that. If this event had not happened, this book may still be on my to-do list.

As open to this idea as I was, it required one of those synchronistic events to confirm this dream and make certain that this portion of my life came to fruition. Now, I will be the first to tell you that as open-minded as I consider myself to be, I still have the tendency to be a little skeptical of things where I have no experience. This case happens to be one of those times when I was unexpectedly opened up even wider than what I thought was possible in spite of my skepticism.

I was involved in one of my many business ventures, at this time, a record label, in which we were promoting an inspirational group. We were asked if the group could perform as a part of some sort of annual church celebration at a church located in Orlando, Florida. This church was headed by a very gracious lady that the people referred to as Prophetess. I briefly met this young lady at the evening celebration after a night of outdoor performances. After our group performed, we were introduced to the Prophetess, at which time she invited us to come back the following morning for the Sunday service. I accepted the invite with some reservations because of my unfamiliarity with this type of church. That evening, we returned to our hotel rooms, and as we prepared to call it a night, I briefly told my two older brothers and my wife that I had been thinking about taking some time off to write a book and asked them what they thought of the idea. This was a very perplexing proposal, considering that I had not too long before just begun reading books on a consistent basis, and I had never really written anything. At any rate, I knew that I wanted to share many of the experiences that I have had throughout this journey that has been my life. At the time, I had no idea what the book would be about. And the more I talked about it, the more I felt it would end up being another one of my great ideas that never came to fruition. That evening as I drifted off to sleep, I thought about whether writing this book was something that I really wanted to take the time to do and if it was in alignment with the direction I wanted my life to ultimately go.

I woke that morning at five before anyone else, convinced somehow that writing this book was what I was supposed to do and that this book was directly in line with my purpose. I immediately woke up my wife and told her my plan to take some time off and begin writing this book. She gave me the response that anyone would have given their spouse at 5:00 a.m., "Sure, honey, that sounds great," and rolled over and went back to sleep. Although this was not the response I'd hoped for, I continued to lay there as my mind raced with ideas of what the book could be about and the manner in which it could possibly be written. I began to drift back off to sleep as a bright image entered into my mind that burned so bright and crystal clear that I immediately thought to myself, *This can't be a dream.* The image was a picture of me on the front of a book cover wearing a dark blue pin stripe suit and a bright red tie. My first thought was, *That's weird* because I would never wear a bright red tie, and my second thought was how illuminated the image was and how clearly I could see all the details of this picture. I could see everything that I had on with great detail, right down to the type of shirt I was wearing and the type of cuff links. I also saw the position of my arms as I stood with them crossed and even the angle in which the camera had been used to capture the shot. Many years later, I can still see this image in my mind just as bright as the first day I saw it. The image I saw that day is the same one that now appears on the front cover of this book (with the exception of the red tie and the folded arms). This was such an unusually clear vision that when I awoke it was the first thing I shared with everyone. I explained to my brothers and my wife about how bright the image was and explained to them all of the details of the picture on the front of this book cover. I told them that it was confirmation that I should start writing this book.

This series of events startled me because of the clarity in which the image had come to me, even though this was not the first time an answer to a question or the solution to a problem had come to me in a dream. But more intriguingly, what took place later that day had never happened before. And it changed my mind about many things, especially the role that this book would play in God's plan for my life.

To set the stage for what happened next, you must understand that I was on my way to a church service that was at a church I had never attended, never even heard of with the exception of the previous night, and most importantly, it was being headed by a lady that people called Prophetess. Now, as spiritually advanced as I thought of myself at that time, I still came from a very small, primitive Baptist church in Huntsville, Alabama, that my mama, my mama's mama, and my mama's mama's mama attended. So to say that I had some reservations and prejudices is an understatement. If you compound that with the fact that I had built a pretty cynical attitude toward organized religion as a whole, I knew we were in for a very interesting day. Like most churches, this one followed the same format from the beginning to end. At the end of service, the young lady that had been introduced as the Prophetess walked to the front of the church and took a seat in a large chair facing the congregation. After a brief prayer led by the Prophetess, she began to go into somewhat of a trancelike state and started to describe things about people that were miraculously in the congregation. As she described these people and what they were going through, one by one they came forward from the congregation. Now, this is not the first time I've seen someone describe a wide range of generalities that could possibly fit anyone and coincidently there was always someone in the congregation who figured that he or she was the subject being talked about and would go into one of those fits. But what made this service a little different was that as these people were drawn to the front of the room through the descriptions, the Prophetess would pray for them and gently tap them on the head and they would fall to the floor in a deep, sleeplike trance. This I had never seen. As I sat and watched this seemingly rehearsed dramatization, I remember laughing inside as I said to myself that there was nothing she could say that would get me to get up in front of all these people, and I sure as hell, under no circumstance, would fall out on the floor. I thought to myself that this was one really clever way to get people to join church. The longer this went on, the more cynical we became, to the point that we were making comments back and forth and even laughing under our breath. This went on for maybe an hour before we began to hear things that sounded startlingly familiar concerning a few of the members of the group that we had brought to perform. Her comments were so precise that we all began to look back and forth in astonishment at the accuracy in which she spoke about two of the members of the group. This got all of our attention, and the giggling immediately stopped as we heard things about people, that we knew she had no way of knowing, being spoken of in such a clear and detailed way. As I watched two of the people that traveled with me go through this process, the experience immediately changed to something personal and very real. As she was seemingly drawing to a close, she continued to sit there in silence with her eyes closed. All of a sudden, she began describing someone that had this special calling in his life and started naming things about him and describing his relationship with the different people he associated with. It only took a few seconds before my dreaded fear came true; I knew that she was now talking about me. She described things about me that she couldn't have read about on a web site or been told because they were things that I had only thought or felt and never divulged to anyone. As much as I heard, I still continued to sit as if she weren't talking about me. In a flash, she opened her eyes and was staring directly at me. She continued to talk, as if to see what was taking me so long to come forward. I immediately dropped my head as I saw the people that were there who knew me all turn to look at me as they heard things that they knew described me. As I continued to look down at the ground, I felt my wife's knee begin to press up against mine while my brother began to push his elbow into my side, as if to say, "Do something." She knew everything from my past. She knew the details of my mother's passing while I was in high school and my constant concern for my two older brothers. She knew about the

56

state of my current and past businesses. The Prophetess even talked about future things that I wanted to do that I had only shared with my brothers and many, many other detailed things that she couldn't have known. She even knew things about my future that I felt were a part of my destiny, but I had never expressed to anyone. But even with all of that, I had convinced myself that I was not going up in front of that church and the several hundred people in attendance. As I listened to some of the things she described, I began to cry as I sat there with my head down. After several minutes, she paused for an extended time, which forced me to eventually look up as I prayed that she was done. Instead she continued to sit there staring directly at me. As I looked away, I saw an old friend that lived in the area, who I had not seen or talked to in a few years, looking right at me, as if to say, "I'm hearing this too." I looked back at the Prophetess as she sat there staring. She looked me in my eyes and said, "By the way, I saw your dream this morning too." She said, "I saw you standing there in your blue, pinstriped suit with your red tie on, staring up at the camera on the cover of your book." Not only did she describe everything about the vision, but she told me that I was going to write this book, and she even told me what the book would be about, something that the dream had not revealed. She told me the book would be about success, but it would be from a spiritual perspective. She even went as far as to call it a ministry that would one day span the globe. At this time, as you can probably imagine, I was floored, and I could no longer contain myself. What they said happened next is still a complete blur to me. I'm told that I got up in front of the church and spoke, confirming what the Prophetess had said, which I do not remember at all. As I left the church that day, everyone was calling me bishop, congratulating me, and telling me that my words confirmed that I was walking in my destiny. Several years later, I began writing this book that the Prophetess had foretold.

The Secret of Life is to Focus on What You Want and Never on That Which You Don't Want

You have to learn to focus on what you want versus that which you don't. Most people do the opposite. We constantly think and talk about what we don't want in the hope that it won't show up. Unfortunately, this is exactly the opposite of what you do if you don't want to have something in particular show up in your life. Unconsciously, we continue this process, and over and over again we end up with exactly the thing that we don't want.

> You have got to focus on growing the grass versus killing the weeds.
>
> —Anonymous

For example, you often hear people describe the type of mate that they would like to attract into their life by describing who they don't want and then they're surprised when that's who keeps showing up. The conversation often sounds like this: "I'm looking for someone who's not afraid to commit." "I don't want another liar," and, "The next person can't be a such and such." All this description does is attract more of what you are describing into your reality. You have to be careful to always focus on what you want and not its opposite. The appropriate conversation would be: "I would like someone who wants to commit, who is honest with me." Or "The next person will be such and such." The above description puts your focus on what you do want and not on the things that you don't want.

This reminds me of a story I read about Mother Teresa that I consider to be the highest example of only focusing on and constantly choosing that which you want versus that which you don't. An anti-war protest was being organized, and the organizer knew that if he could gain the support of Mother Teresa, it would bring worldwide recognition to his cause. Mother Teresa stood as a universal symbol for peace worldwide, and her involvement would undoubtedly raise the consciousness of those involved and generate lots of awareness. When asked, Mother Teresa was honored that they considered her for the key speaker, but she gracefully declined his offer. The organizer asked her why she had declined his invitation to support his antiwar protest since she was someone who was obviously not a supporter of the war. She simply explained that she was not interested in supporting an antiwar movement but asked him to let her know when he had a rally that was for peace, she would gladly be a part of that. Her willingness to participate in a rally that was for peace allowed her to focus on what she wanted, more peace, and not on what she didn't want, which was less war. If she put her attention on less war, she may have gotten it, but that's not what she wanted. Less war is still war, and what she was after was peace, which is the absence of war. It's easy to think that they are the same thing, that more peace is the same as less war. When they are looked at as words on paper or considered as the final results of something, they are the same. But when you look at the process of how you create the end result, they are quite different. What you give your energy to grows. If you put your attention on less war, war will expand and continue to exist. If you put your attention on more peace, peace will expand and continue to exist. In this particular desire, the words *more* or *less* do not receive the energy; therefore, the words *peace* or *war* are energized and end up expanding. Mother Teresa put her attention and energy toward what she wanted (peace) versus what she didn't want (war). Clearly, she was operating from the premise that what you focus on expands and what you resist will persist.

As you arm yourself with this information, you can now begin to put your attention on the things that you want to come into your life versus the things that you don't. This is what is meant by the old adage, "When it rains, it pours." What this saying is referencing is that when things begin to go a certain way, good or bad, we tend to accelerate it by focusing on the direction that it's already headed.

This has always been my experience. Every time I place my full attention on what I am after and not on the opposite, all types of synchronistic and miraculous things begin to show up that catapult me toward the achievement of it. The opposite is also true; every time I've placed my attention on something I didn't want, I got exactly that.

The house I described in the test in the introduction of this book that put me over the top to hit my one-million-dollar mark is a great example of this. When I was focused on what I wanted, one million dollars by my thirty-fourth birthday, all things magically lined up and created that experience even without my involvement. The investment home that I purchased with a partner for 505K had an after-repair value of 1.2 million. It needed about 100K in renovations, which, with all things considered, would place me a little above the one-million-dollar goal, including my partner's portion of the profits. What's amazing about this deal was that when it was placed under contract and in my control I had no idea how I was going to go about purchasing this house and what it would entail to make this deal work.

> Everything you want is out there waiting for you to ask. Everything you want also wants you. But you have to take action to get it.
>
> —Jack Canfield[19]

After all, I had only seen the property once in a brief walk-through and in photographs someone else took.

As I completed the necessary paperwork to have such a large renovation project completed, things just seemed to fall in place. All of the finances, contractors, and everything else needed to complete this transaction fell into place like clockwork. And sure enough, a month later, the house was purchased and the renovation began.

Midway through the project, two unrelated and strange things happened. As I look back, they were obviously part of this process. First, my wife stopped by one day to see this project that I had been working on. She loved the house, and at the same time, my partner decided that he wanted out of the project. So I told my wife to put our house on the market for sale just to see what would happen. Within one week, the house was under contract, and two weeks later, the house was sold with an unexpected move-in date of one week. For anyone who has ever sold a house before I'm certain you would agree you have not heard of that happening very often.

Meanwhile, the renovations on the house project were far from complete. But the houses in the neighborhood that I lived in were taking six months or longer to sell, so I knew we couldn't wait. If we were going to sell, then this was the time. We accepted the offer, sold our house, and immediately started making custom changes to the renovation plans of our project home now that we intended to live there. This experience made me realize that it all started to fall into place the moment I became clear about what I wanted. I believe that this is true for anyone who's ever accomplished anything.

When you look at the lives of the people who have made the biggest impact on our world, they knew what they wanted, and regardless of the obstacles, they were able to achieve it. I'm reminded of a story I read in the book *Awaken the Genius* about Albert Einstein. I thought it was worth repeating here as an example of great achievement in spite of seemingly insurmountable odds.

Albert Einstein didn't even graduate from high school, and he actually failed an examination that would have allowed him to pursue a career as an electrical engineer. Yet, he still became one of the greatest scientists of our time. How did he accomplish this? Well, in 1896 he was accepted into Zurich Polytechnic and graduated as a secondary school teacher of mathematics and physics. His first two years after graduation, were lean ones, but he finally obtained a position at a Swiss patent office. The work was tedious and demanding, yet while employed there he completed an extraordinary range of publications in theoretical physics. These texts were all written in his spare time and with no outside contact with the scientific or literary communities of the time. He later submitted one of these scientific papers to the University of Zurich and was granted a doctorate degree on its merit. The next year he was granted an appointment as associate professor of physics at the University of Zurich.

—Patrick Kelly Porter[20]

In the short span of thirteen years, Einstein progressed from a primary-level education to recognition as a leading scientific thinker. What was his secret? He knew what he wanted and was determined to get it.

You Have Everything You Need To Get What You Want

Whatever you need to become who you are meant to be—when you consciously decide to walk in your destiny—will be provided for you. When you observe Michael Jordan and all of his accomplishments, there is a little-known fact that pervades most of the stats that you hear about that I feel is the most important one. His six-foot-six-inch height and body design cannot be explained based on anyone in his family history. No man in his family's known history—his father, grandfather, great grandfather, or any other family member—stood over six feet tall. When his father was asked how he could explain this phenomenon, he responded that (after he checked the mailman) he realized that every now and then you see someone and you have to say to yourself that he must have been born to do what he does. Michael Jordan's height came from his desire to be the greatest basketball player in modern-day history. After he decided what he wanted and became clear about it, the universe provided him with the things that he needed, especially the things that he could not control but were necessary for him to accomplish his ultimate goal.

Something Has to Change

You really do either have to change who you are or change what you want. So we must begin the process of identifying what we truly want and make all the necessary changes in ourselves that will allow us to accomplish it. Each of the seven truths contained in these pages are designed to help you make the changes you need in order to get the things you desire. Now that you have the tools that you need to help identify your purpose, you can begin to change your wants into a desire. Your burning desire will bring you clarity on this matter, and you will then be able to change that desire into a choosing. This is the manifesting principle behind this truth. Choose to have and live your purpose and nothing else, and you will see just how simple success for you can be.

Once you have decided what you are consciously choosing to experience in your life, you must get beyond the second roadblock, which is disbelief.

Simply, most people don't believe they can have it. Their beliefs about the achievement of what they want are in conflict with the very thing they are after. This dilemma must be addressed before the manifesting process can truly begin. This brings us to the second truth. You must develop beliefs that are in support of what it is that you now choose for yourself. Therefore, before you can develop beliefs that support you having what you are now choosing, you have to first discover what you ultimately would like to have present in your life. Then your next step is to purposefully design beliefs that support you having what you have just identified.

Truth #2

You must develop beliefs that are in
support of you getting what you want.

- Application: After identifying what you want, you must then choose beliefs that are in support of you having it.

- Explanation: You must make certain that the beliefs you hold concerning what you have now identified as what you want are in support of those things. We often find that the biggest reason we haven't gotten what we want is that our beliefs about it are not in support of us getting it. We usually find that we don't believe that we can achieve what we want, and this must change if we ever plan on having it.

- Manifesting Principle: The highest form of a supporting belief is a supporting attitude. Changing from beliefs that support what you want to an attitude that supports it is the quickest way to manifest it.

  These truths used together will design your life plan for manifesting:

  Truth #1: The first step to getting what you want is to identify what it is that you want.

  Truth #2: You must develop beliefs that are in support of you getting what you want.

Now that you understand the manifesting power of defining what you want and becoming clear about your intentions of achieving it, developing beliefs that are in support of it will cause you to experience having it faster than any actions you can take. Many people have lived great lives just by becoming clear about truth number one, but those that have developed this second truth, whether consciously or not, have purposefully participated in the design of their lives.

What the mind can conceive and believe, it can achieve.

—*Napoleon Hill*[21]

What do you believe?

Over the years, you have probably heard all types of things about belief, so much so that most people have placed the power of belief somewhere between false hope and wishful thinking. Have you heard people say things like, "Whatever you believe, you can achieve" and then wondered why the things you believe have not been achieved?

Opinions are the cheapest commodities on earth—everyone has one.

—Napoleon Hill[22]

Undoubtedly, it is true that believing you can achieve your heart's desire is essential; however, most people don't know what they believe. This is mainly due to the fact that most of our beliefs are not even ours; they are the beliefs of our parents, friends, co-workers, pastors, and the very powerful and suggestive advertisers. You must develop your own set of self-supportive beliefs to take you closer to the things you want instead of toward the things you don't want. How many times has someone that you care about, who also cares about you, told you that you couldn't do something you wanted to do or not to get your hopes up too high about something that you really wanted?

Whether you think you can or can't, you are right.
—Henry Ford[23]

It's not that this person is trying to hurt you; most likely, he or she is actually trying to protect you from being hurt or let down because his or her beliefs about you achieving what you want differ from your beliefs. I once heard someone say in a seminar I attended that it isn't the thief with the knife or gun that will rob you of your dreams, but instead it's the friend or family member who says that it can't be done. For this reason, you must learn to "become independent of the good opinion of other people."[24] It is very essential that you learn to develop your own opinions and beliefs about the things you want, and you must be able to separate yourself from the beliefs and opinions of others.

This above all: to thine own self be true.
—William Shakespeare[25]

Not even your mother can tell you what's best for you; only you can. No one truly knows the deep burning desires of your heart; only you do. You must learn to hear from yourself because no one knows you better than you. However, this can only be true if you take the time to discover your own beliefs and make certain that you rid yourself of others, especially if they are not in support of what you want. Now, I often say this to people, and the most common response I hear is, "That's easier said than done."

Someone's perception of you doesn't have to become your reality. It's your perception of you that's your realty. That's why you must work on you.
—Anonymous

When people place too much value on the opinions of those around them, they find it very difficult to become independent of those opinions. And this is exactly what must happen in order to break free of the restrictions placed on you by others via their opinions about you. Most people don't realize just how much what other people think of them dictates what they do and don't do and how these restrictions directly affect what they could potentially become. The problem with this is if the person whose opinion you respect is wrong, but you believe that they are right, because of your relationship with them, you will become just what they thought you would rather than what you could have become. Then they say to you, "See, I told you it would have ended up this way had you tried to do what you were intending to do." This reassures them and you that they were right. Thus, they will continue this damaging behavior, and you will begin to look for opportunities to do the same. This vicious cycle is the single most debilitating and restrictive thing that takes place in the lives of most people. When a person becomes just what those around him expected of him, rather than what he wanted, he usually ends up leading a life that's unfulfilling. And in turn, he becomes resentful of the life that others have chosen for him.

I had a friend who despised the profession that the women in her family had chosen as their careers. Even though her father was in the same profession, it was her mother and older sister's opinion she respected the most. She would often comment that she hated everything about their profession, how it aged her mother and how it made her sister seem old and unhappy (her sister was still in her early thirties). She resented the fact that her mother had convinced her sister to follow in her footsteps and thus ended up throwing away all of her dreams to become exactly what her mother wanted her to be. The fact that her mother's opinion dominated her sister's life to the point that her sister had become the exact same responsible, old, and boring person that her mother was troubled her greatly. She vowed that this would not be her fate and that she would never throw away her dreams of becoming what she desired. She had already been recognized as a brilliant and very talented person in her desired field; therefore, the sky was truly the limit for her. I saw her many years later, and from the moment I saw her, I knew immediately that she had become the exact person that she had despised growing up. I didn't have to even inquire as to what profession she had chosen to pursue, for I saw the very grown-up and unhappy person that she once accused her sister of being. I later heard that she had become the exact same thing that her mother was, and she had even surpassed her mother's level of success in the profession that she once despised. Now, I'm sure that her mother could not have been more proud, and I'm certain that at some point this became part of her decision to stop living her life and chose the life that those around her chose for her. Most likely, this will eventually lead to her despising either herself, her mother, or maybe even both. This is typically the end result when what you choose for yourself is dictated by what someone else desires for you. Equally as important as not becoming the victim of this type of scenario is not inflicting this abuse on someone else. Your choosing for someone what they chose for themselves, whether you are in agreement or not, is the surest indicator of unconditional love. A passage from *Conversations with God* sums it up best in this way: "God chooses your highest good for you, but above that he chooses your will for you. And this is the surest measure of love."[26] When I want for you what you want for you, then I truly love you. When I want for you what I want for you, then I love myself through you. This is the measure of whether you love others and if others love you. [26]

> I am replacing my desire for power over others with my efforts to understand and master myself in any and all situations. The things I love, I have to learn to leave alone.
> —Dr. Wayne Dyer[27]

Knowing what you want can be a very difficult thing if you've never taken the time to figure it out. And uncovering your true beliefs to determine if they support what you want can be even more difficult. But once figured out, the combination of the two can be the most liberating and success-generating accomplishment you have ever achieved. Nevertheless, most people don't realize that not mastering this ability is a major reason why they don't attract the things they want into their lives. But when you think about it, it's easy to see that if your beliefs about what you want are not in support of you getting it, then your chances of achieving it will be drastically reduced. For this reason, this truth comes behind truth number one and precedes all of the other truths. You must get this one right before the others will work for you. How many times have you said that you wanted to have a certain thing only to later turn around and talk yourself out of it because you didn't believe that you could get it? If you don't believe that you can have the things you want, how will you ever get them? This second truth is known by all those who have ever accomplished anything and could be just as easily identified by those who have suffered defeat if they took the time to reflect on why. It all starts with what your beliefs are and whether they're in support of what you want or their opposites.

So how does one change one's beliefs or make certain that they are their own and support what one wants? To do this, you must first differentiate between your beliefs and the beliefs of others. This will help you discover your true beliefs on any subject. As you think of each subject matter that is important to you, begin to monitor what beliefs you hold about it and write it down without second-guessing or forming any judgments about it. To help get this process flowing, ask yourself thought-provoking questions regarding your beliefs about each subject matter, questions like, "Do I believe that I deserve to have what I'm pursuing?" and "Do I have what it takes to succeed at what I'm pursuing?" These are questions that will get you going in the right direction.

Initially all of your thoughts about your beliefs may sound supporting, but continue to dig deeper with more penetrating questions like, "If who I am could get me what I wanted, then why don't I already have it?" and "What beliefs do I carry that have kept me from getting what I've wanted in the past?" If you are creative and continue to ask yourself more and more in-depth questions, you will quickly move past the surface and enter uncharted territory. Remember that the size of the questions always determines the size of the answer. Once you have written down all of the beliefs that come to mind, read each belief and ask yourself, "Does holding this belief bring me closer to accomplishing my goal or take me farther away?" As you go through this exercise, take the sheet of paper and place an *S* next to any belief that you believe supports you in getting what you want and an *X* next to the beliefs that don't.

To be certain that each belief serves you in getting what you are pursuing, you should run a quick test in kinesiology to determine which beliefs are truly supportive and which are not.

Kinesiology is the study of muscles and their movements, as applied to physical conditioning. This way of testing has long established that: when you are in the presence of physical stimuli that is good for you then your body's muscles become strengthened, and when presented with a stimuli that is not good, the opposite phenomenon happens, your muscles become weak. In the late 70s, Dr. John Diamond refined this specialty into a new discipline he called *Behavioral Kinesiology*. Dr. Diamond's startling discovery was that indicator muscles would strengthen or weaken in the presence of positive or negative emotional and intellectual stimuli, as well as physical stimuli. Dr. Diamond outlined this study in his 1979 book, *Your Body Doesn't Lie.*[28]

Picking up where Dr. Diamond left off, Dr. David Hawkins spent thirty years expanding this work, and what he found was even more startling then what had been previously discovered. He found that this process could be applied to anything regardless of the source of the stimuli, including but not limited to things nonphysical, like thoughts and beliefs.[29] Here's what he wrote in his book *Power vs. Force:*

The basic function of any measuring device is simply to give a signal indicating the detection by the instrument of slight change. The body can discern, to the finest degree, the difference between that which is in support of life and that which is not. This isn't surprising: After all, living things react positively to what is life-supporting and negatively to what is not; this is a fundamental mechanism of survival.[30]

In Dr. Hawkins medical study, test subjects ranged from what the world calls normal to severely ill psychiatric patients. Subjects were tested in Canada, the United States, Mexico, and throughout South America, Northern Europe, and the Far East. They were of all nationalities, ethnic backgrounds and religions, ranging in age from children to elders in their 90's, and covered a wide spectrum of physical and emotional health. Subjects were tested individually and in groups by many different testers and groups of testers. But in all cases, without exception, the results were identical and entirely reproducible, fulfilling the fundamental requirement of the scientific method.

To begin the testing procedure, two people are required. One acts as test subject, by holding out one arm laterally (parallel to the ground). As you hold thoughts in your mind, the second person then presses down with two fingers on the wrist of the extended arm and says, "Resist." The subject then resists the downward pressure with all his strength. That's all there is to it. This test was done on thousands of subjects and was infallible; It worked 100% of the times tested.[31]

Now, how does this apply to your figuring out which beliefs empower you and which ones do not? The beliefs, that you possess, that help you grow stronger, are beliefs that are in support of you and should be written down on a separate sheet of paper. The beliefs that you possess that cause you to go weak, should be written on a separate sheet of paper. Each of these sections should be kept for specific reasons. Those beliefs that support you will be read daily, and those that don't will be changed through a process, later described, involving changes in attitude and how to ceremonially discard those beliefs. Bad beliefs have to be replaced, like bad habits, with good beliefs.

Proper belief is rooted in proper attitude. Therefore, a positive attitude precedes positive beliefs. Many people believe that their thoughts about a subject are generally their beliefs about it. Nothing could be further from the truth. Your thoughts jump around and are influenced by more outside sources than anything else so this can never be a good barometer for belief. It's your attitude towards a particular subject that mostly shapes your beliefs about it. No matter how positive you try to be about the beliefs that you hold for yourself, if your attitude towards something is not in support of it then its achievement is impossible.

> Nothing can stop the man with the right mental attitude from achieving his goal. Nothing on earth can help the man with the wrong mental attitude.
>
> —Thomas Jefferson[32]

Therefore, your attitude is what determines your beliefs. The highest form of belief is attitude. Your attitude is the bigger, grander version of your belief. Your attitude encompasses your belief. It steers you in the direction toward the beliefs that should be retained as your own. As you come in contact with different beliefs, some yours but most not, it's your attitude that will dictate which ones you accept as your own and those you will let pass. If your attitude toward a particular subject is positive, when your beliefs are confronted with a new idea about it that is also positive, you will most likely accept it. And the same is true if you have a negative attitude about something. You will be attracted to the beliefs that support your attitude about that subject. This is the power of having a positive attitude. You attract thoughts that are a reflection of your attitude. The more positive your attitude is about something, the more instances that will begin to show up in your life that reinforce what you believe about it and vice versa. Your attitude will dictate your beliefs, and your beliefs will then reinforce your attitude. I always thought that it was not known which one comes first, just like the chicken or the egg. But through this process, I've discovered that attitude precedes belief. Belief is like a large chunk of clay; it can be shaped and molded to fit any form and attitude is the hand that shapes it. It's the larger perspective. Many beliefs can be held inside of one attitude. In other words, you can hold many beliefs about a particular subject, but it is your attitude that determines if they are positive, negative, in support of, or not. Your attitude toward a thing directly shapes your beliefs about it. If you have a negative attitude toward the attainment of something you want, then your belief that you can have it will also be negative. And the opposite is true as well.

The pessimist borrows trouble; the optimist lends encouragement.

—William Arthur Ward[33]

Of course, there is more to it than just trying to be positive or having a positive attitude about things. You must learn to have a positive attitude about everything that you want to have in your life and attempt not to have any attitude, positive or negative, toward the things that you don't want in your life. If you take the advice being offered here, you will only focus on the things that you want and not on those that you don't. Therefore, if you choose to have a positive attitude in support of something, then nothing else remains. This is because you have already agreed to only focus on what you want. You may now be thinking, *How can I have an attitude that's positive and supports what I want and not have its opposite (what I don't want) show up?* The answer is twofold. First, change your attitude in total support of what you want. Subsequently, all of your beliefs about it will change and the manifesting process will begin. Secondly, you have to develop the ability to eradicate your beliefs and attitude about the things you don't want. You accomplish this by losing your opinion about it. If there is some aspect of your life that you don't want to continue to manifest, you must change your attitude about it and then your beliefs and then abandon your opinion all together. You must reverse the previous process described earlier in this chapter regarding changing your beliefs by changing your attitude. Understanding and mastering this one truth will transport you quantum leaps toward the development and achievement of your goals. This is the reason why your attitude is the manifesting principle behind the second truth. Mastering this manifesting principle will permit you to bypass the need to exchange unsupportive beliefs with ones that are, primarily because anything that comes into the sphere of this larger supporter of you will be rejected simply on the premise that it doesn't fall in line with your larger, grander attitude about it. This larger perspective, once directed in support of what you want, produces its manifestation versus its creation. For instance, if one says, "I believe that I can live cancer free," that could be considered a change in belief; however, a change in attitude would be, "My body is perfect, and only health and wellness can exist in it." You see, this type of change in attitude not only rules out cancer, but it also encompasses any other ailment without ever naming or changing a belief about a particular disease. This allows you to focus only on what you desire and never say, think, or do anything that directs energy to something that you don't desire.

I often tell people that your attitude makes up 100 percent of what it takes to be successful, and I can prove it 100 percent of the time because it is that infallible. Often, people are so bombarded with things disguising themselves as the truth that it's hard to hear someone say that something is the absolute truth and that it can be proven beyond a shadow of a doubt. But that is what I'm saying, so here we go. If you believe, as I do, that we live in a perfect universe and that there are no accidents, then this will really drive home that point. Just like the kinesiology test, this example represents another one of those infallible truths.

Let's perform a little experiment with the alphabet, which uncovers a magical relationship to truth number two. First of all, the history of the alphabet began in Ancient Egypt more than a millennium into the history of writing.[34] The first pure alphabet emerged around 2000 BCE to represent the language of Semitic workers in Egypt and was derived from the alphabetic principles of the Egyptian hieroglyphs.[35] Almost all alphabets in the world today either descended directly from this development, like the Greek and Roman alphabets, or they were inspired by its design.[36] Interestingly, with the sole exception of Korea's Hangul script, all of today's major alphabets have a common origin.[37] Therefore, what is true for one is true for them all.

Now, to begin this experiment, you will need to start by writing

the word *attitude* vertically on a sheet of paper. Then write the entire
alphabet across the top of that sheet of paper. When you look at the
alphabet, it's easy to see that the first letter of the alphabet is an *A*.
So, next to the letter *A* in *attitude,* write the number one. The second
letter is *T,* which is the twentieth letter, so next to the letter *T,* write
the number twenty. And you do this for the entire word. I encourage
you to count the letters yourself to make certain that my math has
not deteriorated since my days in school. Once all of the numerical
values corresponding to the letters are counted and added up, you
will see they equal one hundred exactly. Just in case you need to see
this example written out, here it is below:[38]

A	B	C	D	E	F	G	H	I	J	K	L	M
1	2	3	4	5	6	7	8	9	10	11	12	13

N	O	P	Q	R	S	T	U	V	W	X	Y	Z
14	15	16	17	18	19	20	21	22	23	24	25	26

A	T	T	I	T	U	D	E		
1	20	20	9	20	21	4	5	=	100

This is just one little example of how the universe displays its unde-
niable perfection and proves that the proper attitude is 100 percent
of what it takes to have success at anything.

So how do you fix the fact that you know what you want but
don't truly believe you can achieve it or deserve it? The first step is be
open to accepting the fact that some of the beliefs that you hold dear
and feel strongly about may be erroneous (untrue or with error). This
should be a little easier to do now that you've come to realize that it's
a good possibility that many of your beliefs are not even your own.
The very fact that most of your beliefs were given to you by your
parents, family members, and close friends may help you ascertain
that many of the beliefs you currently have maybe untrue for you.
The poem below illustrates this idea brilliantly.

The Cookie Thief

A woman was waiting at the airport one night, with several
long hours before her flight,
    She hunted a book in the airport shop, bought a bag
of cookies and found a place to drop. She was engrossed
in her book, but happen to see that the gentleman next to
her as bold as can be, grab a cookie or two from the bag in
between, which she tried to ignore to avoid a scene. As the
minutes ticked by she watched the clock as the gutsy cookie
thief diminished her stock. With each one she took, he took
one too. When only one was left she wondered what he'd
do. With a smile on his face and a nervous laugh he took the
last cookie and broke it in half. He offered her half as he ate
the other; she snatched it and thought "oh brother." Why
this guy has some nerve and he's also rude, why he didn't
even show any gratitude? She had never known when she
had been so gauled, and sighed with relief when her flight
was called. She gathered her things and headed to the gate
refusing to look back at that thieving ingrate.
    She boarded the plane and sank in her seat
    Then sought her book which was almost complete.
    As she reached in her baggage she gasped with surprise
    There was her bag of cookies in front of her eyes.
    "If mine are here" she moaned with despair
    "Then the others were his and he tried to share"
    "Too late to apologize she realized with grief."
    That she was the rude one, the ingrate, the thief.

—Valerie Cox[39]

This poem was first published in the book
    Chicken Soup for the Soul by Jack Canfield and Mark Victor Hansen.

As you read this poem, you should recognize how this type of thing, in perhaps a little less dramatic fashion, has happened in your life at some time or another. Life has a way of teaching us these little lessons that we need in order to grow ourselves in the direction of our desires. It's during the times when our current set of beliefs is challenged that we have the greatest chance for growth. Now, I will be the first to say that just because something challenges your beliefs doesn't mean that it's a new belief that you must adopt. Sometimes things challenge your set of beliefs in a way that adds confirmation and reinforces your current set. This is the way you must approach this portion of discovering your beliefs and attitudes toward your desires. You must approach it with the open-mindedness and discernment that must be present in order for growth and change to occur. Once you are open to the possibility of acquiring some new beliefs and you now know what your beliefs are, it's time to put this new information to work for you.

I'm certain that discovering your beliefs about achieving what you desire is as much of a real eye-opener for you (if you did the exercise) as it was for me. This is where most people face their toughest challenge. Many times, what is learned during this process is that the very things we say we desire most are the things that we believe are not good for us or to us. Whether this is taught to us by someone else or learned through our experiences, we often find that our desires are things that make us feel bad for wanting them. Some people have been taught to feel this way because they find that what they desire and what others desire for them are not the same things. Whenever we are faced with this dilemma, it usually involves the people that we love and the people whose opinions we value the most. If it weren't someone we held dear, we probably would care less about what they thought in the first place.

Naturally, this is a very difficult situation to be in because no matter what you choose in this situation, someone is going to end up unhappy. The only difference is the disappointment this may cause your friend, family member, or spouse will, in most cases, last only for a season, but yours will last for all of your seasons. For this reason, I encourage people to always go with what they know deep down inside is right for them, even if it's not easy and no one else agrees. Otherwise, when we habitually sacrifice our heart's desires or inner yearnings for fear of disappointing or offending a loved one's perceptions of what is best for us, we slowly begin to learn not to trust ourselves and go with what others want. Perhaps an equally damaging and self-defeating behavior is choosing to do what others want and being rewarded for it. Here again we are being taught to please others rather than pleasing ourselves. This is how most of our beliefs become our beliefs. Through this process of acceptance, influence, and discouragement of our opinions by those closest to us, our beliefs are born.

The next way our beliefs are taught to us is through interaction with our peer groups, the education system, and other people in authority. This process continues throughout childhood and often into adulthood. Until our experiences and feelings stop aligning with what those around us are teaching us, we tend not to question what we are being taught directly or indirectly.

For many, adolescence is a turning point. During this period, people begin to question what they are being taught, especially if it is directly in conflict with their experiences and, more importantly, with what their feelings are telling them. Nonetheless, it is during this period of time that most people decide to suppress what they feel and go along with the program.

Occasionally, there are those who choose to rewrite the program to fit what they believe is true for them. Depending upon when you awaken to this realization, the temperament of those around you, such as your parents or guardians, your spouse, friends, etc., directly determines the outcome of how or whether you are successful on this path. Most people go through life fluctuating between doing it their way sometimes and the way others think they should—pushing at times and being pushed at other times, directing sometimes and being lead at others. As this push and pull, up and down game of tug a war continues to fluctuate, so does one's success. It's only when the pain of where you are begins to outweigh the pain of taking the necessary steps toward where you desire to go do you then and only then move past this (sometimes) self-taught, self-defeating behavior. To overcome this you will have to dig deep to find your own set of truths that you can begin to apply regardless of what those around you say. Although this is tough to remedy, after a few short cycles of letting someone else's beliefs dominate your success, you will eventually self-fix the minute you recognize who or what the culprit is.

We tend to get what we expect.

—Norman Vincent Peale[40]

However, there is a more deeply rooted belief that most people suffer from that is not so easily fixed. This belief has to be corrected in order for the process of manifestation to begin to work for you. This is where our root beliefs of what is good and bad come into conflict with what we have been taught, mainly by those who wish to suppress us, either consciously or unconsciously, and with what we know deep down inside is true for us. Have you ever asked yourself why everything that seems to be good to you is always somehow bad for you? How could you be wrong about everything that feels right to you? Do you really believe that in all of God's perfection that we are the greatest of creations, yet we do not possess the ability to think and decide what's best for ourselves? The problem is, over time, we are taught that everything we desire is bad—money is bad, success is bad, and desiring more is bad. And unless you feel like you are also bad, you will always be in conflict because if you intrinsically feel like you are good, then why do you desire bad things? Do you see how this conflict of good and bad could send you into the wrong direction? This is the reason why the people you call "bad" always seem to get the things that they want while the people you would consider "good" often struggle. It's because we have been taught that most of the things we want are bad, and if you are a good person and desire them, then there is a conflict. This is also the reason why people who do things that they hate have no problem demanding top dollar, and when we see this we say, "they deserve it." Yet for the people who do what they love and make a ton of money doing it, we become leery of them and begin to resent them. The first group seems to be getting bad for bad and this is okay, but the second group seems to be getting bad for good, and we can't figure out why. In actuality, some people hold such conflicting beliefs and this makes it very difficult for them to manifest abundance. Many misguidedly think you should have to sacrifice something dear to receive abundance and others believe you must reject abundance to be spiritual or serve God. Therefore, some people have a hard time accepting lots of money for doing good things and others have a hard time paying for it. This is the very reason why people have problems with the pastor's of megachurches. Some people view it as bad to receive money for doing something good, like what it takes to build a large church. Anyone in any other profession who built a large successful organization like a major church would expect to be paid top dollar and no one would argue. But if a pastor demands top dollar for building a church, all hell breaks loose.

I never realized this to be true until my brothers and I started what we called a success system that taught real estate investing and wealth-building principles to anyone who desired to learn, and this was done through weekly conference calls, 100 percent free of charge. You would not believe the type of resistance and scrutiny this venture was met with because we were doing something that was perceived as good and wanted nothing in exchange (another good). Therefore, it was assumed that we had to be up to something bad. It became so ridiculous that we eventually had to start charging a fee before people felt comfortable receiving what we were giving away to them free of charge. As unfortunate as it sounds, this is a true story, and it happens to organizations whose intention is to operate from what is most true for them rather than from what others in society would teach you as being true. Do you see how this conflict in our root beliefs has manifested itself all throughout our society and is playing itself out in your life? Are you normally skeptical when someone offers you something free of charge or for less than what you perceive the value should be? This is a symptom of the type of error in belief that keeps most people from achieving their dreams. To remedy this, we must do our own self-evaluation to discover what our truest beliefs are regarding what is good and bad in correlation to the things you desire. This must be done internally because this is where your highest truths ultimately reside. So do yourself a favor and don't seek outside council on this matter, regardless of how important that person's opinion is to you. Remember, no one knows what is ultimately best for you better than you, not your spouse, best friend, or even your pastor. Most of these relationships are the source of your misguided root beliefs in the first place. Nonetheless, I will leave this for your own discovery and discernment.

> Yet he who reigns within himself and rules his passions, desires, and fears is more than a king.
> —John Milton[41]

After six months of digging deep to discover my own life's purpose and getting that part of my plan past me, I realized that my beliefs about what I identified as my truest desires were in direct conflict with one another. It was not that I didn't believe that I could accomplish what I wanted; it was actually the exact opposite. I really believed that I was born to do what I wanted to do. The underlying problem with this belief was a lot more subtle and much harder to identify. My belief was that what I wanted would cause me to spend too much time away from my family, therefore neglecting those who matter most in my life. I developed a poor attitude toward that which I wanted and procrastinated when it came time to do the things necessary to achieve my desires. This, I soon found, could be easily fixed. All I had to do was broaden my beliefs enough to include the possibility that my success would enable me to take my family with me, which is what I truly desired. At that point, I felt I was in the clear. Having this second truth answered would put me on the path toward my achieving my heart's desires.

As I started working with this newfound clarity, I began to realize that there was something else in my belief system that was affecting my attitude in ways that kept my desires at bay. It was through the process described earlier of continued questioning that I began to uncover my most buried beliefs about what I wanted and what was keeping me from having an attitude that was supportive of it. On a very subconscious level, I held the belief that all those who had come before me and attempted to make the type of change in the world that I desired had all died violently in the prime of their lives and left spouses and young kids behind. It was this underlining belief that for years held me hostage by generating the fear of what might become of me if I pursued my destiny. As I explored this fear, I soon realized that it was this belief that had undermined many of my plans in life and had paralyzed me in many instances. This underlining belief had shaped many of the decisions in my life regarding when I would marry, have children, and many other major events, including whether or not I would pursue my purpose. I knew that I was at a crossroad, and in order for these truths to work in my life, I would have to overcome this belief and develop a new set of beliefs that would get me what I wanted rather than that which I desperately did not. I was actually killing my desires for what I wanted. How could I have a red-hot burning desire to achieve something that I knew deep down inside would ultimately bring me what I feared the most? At that instant, I remembered something I read once, that fear and faith were the same thing. This statement said that fear is the belief in something negative and faith is the belief in something positive. This idea led me to discover that it wasn't just a change in belief that was needed. Instead I needed a change in attitude, and the proper attitude toward what I wanted would create the change I needed in my belief. I knew that the right attitude would force me to feed my faith, and if I did, my doubts would starve to death. This is how the process of creation works. *Once you decide what you desire, you must identify an attitude that supports its accomplishment.*

Creation

All things that happen to you in your life have been created by you on some level. You create on three different levels. First, you create by your attitude and beliefs about the things you care about. Your beliefs and attitudes are more important than what you think, speak, or do. This is why creation, on a personal level, starts here because it is impossible to think, speak, or do something that you don't believe. Secondly, you can easily believe something yet have a negative attitude toward your achievement of it and, in turn, receive the exact opposite result hoped for. This is what was happening to me; I was canceling myself out. Before you have a thought, speak a word, or take an action, something precedes these things and sets the direction that things will flow. Some people call this your sponsoring thought, but I like to refer to it as your sponsoring attitude. It's a pretty established fact that what you think about repeatedly, you will eventually talk about, and what you talk about, you will act upon, and what you act upon repeatedly becomes a habit. Your habits will determine your character, and your character is who you are. However, what's not often talked about is what precedes this. It's your attitude and beliefs that set the tone for the results of this creative process. If you have a negative attitude toward a particular thing, then the thoughts you have will also be. And if your thoughts are negative, then so will be your words because we know that one comes from the other. And thus you will take the wrong actions and get the wrong results.

The second way you create is by selecting your internal response to external events. In such instances, you may not have initiated the event, but you still have the ability to choose the type of attitude to approach it with. This will determine how you will think, speak, react, and ultimately the experiences that will result from this event. An example of this is when you hear the stories of something terrible happening to someone and he or she somehow takes the lemons he or she was dealt and makes lemonade.

One of the greatest examples of this is the life of Nelson Mandela.

Nelson Rolihlahla Mandela was born in a village near Umtata in the Transkei on July 18, 1918. His father was the principal councilor to the Acting Paramount Chief of Thembuland. After his father's death, the young Mandela became the Paramount Chief's ward to be groomed to assume high office. However, influenced by the cases that came before the Chief's court, he decided to become a lawyer.

During the entire decade of the 1950's, Mandela was the victim of various forms of repression. He was banned, arrested, and imprisoned. Forced to live apart from his family, moving from place to place to evade detection by the government's ubiquitous informers and police spies, Mandela had to adopt a number of disguises. He sometimes dressed as a common laborer, at other times as a chauffeur; his successful evasion of the police earned him the title of the Black Pimpernel.

Not long after his return to South Africa, Mandela was arrested and charged with illegal exit from the country, and incitement to strike. Mandela was convicted and sentenced to five years imprisonment. While serving his sentence he was charged, in the Rivonia Trial, with sabotage. Mandela was sentenced to life imprisonment and started his prison years in the notorious Robben Island Prison, a maximum security prison on a small island 7Km off the coast near Cape Town. In April 1984 he was transferred to Pollsmoor Prison in Cape Town and in December 1988 he was moved to the Victor Verster Prison near Paarl from where he was eventually released. While in prison, Mandela flatly rejected offers made by his jailers for remission of his sentence, in exchange for accepting the Bantustan policy by recognizing the independence of the Transkei and agreeing to settle there. Again in the 1980's, Mandela rejected an offer of release on the condition that he renounce violence. "Prisoners cannot enter into contracts, only free men can negotiate," he said.

Released on February 11, 1990, Mandela plunged wholeheartedly into his life's work, striving to attain the goals he and others had set almost four decades earlier. In 1991, at the first national conference of the ANC, held inside South Africa after being banned for decades, Nelson Mandela was elected President.

Nelson Mandela has never wavered in his devotion to democracy, equality, and learning. Despite terrible provocation, he has never answered racism with racism. His life has been an inspiration, in South Africa and throughout the world, to all who are oppressed and deprived and to all who are opposed to oppression and deprivation.

In a life that symbolizes the triumph of the human spirit over man's inhumanity to man, Nelson Mandela accepted the 1993 Nobel Peace Prize on behalf of all South Africans who suffered and sacrificed so much to bring peace to our land. Also, Mandela has received honorary degrees from more than 50 international universities and is chancellor of the University of the North. He retired from Public life in June 1999 and currently resides in his birthplace, Qunu, Transkei.[42]

Stories such as these teach us that we can have control over those events that happen to us that we feel we don't control simply by choosing the right attitude.

The third level of creating underlies events that seemingly happen all around you. You are involved in or a part of them but not overtly in control of them. Only a select group of people acknowledges any control over this part of creation. In these situations, something happens and you end up feeling that it worked out just as you hoped it would. Or you may regard it as a coincidence that certain things seem to line up to bring about a certain outcome. Some may consider such events as a blessing, good luck, or even fate. On the other hand, if it was not the desired outcome hoped for, then there's a tendency to refer to it as punishment, bad luck, karma, or even a curse from God.

Just a small percentage of people feel they have any control over this level of creation. This third level of creation is comprised of events that are usually categorized as natural disasters, accidents, things that happen to groups of people that are attributed to them being in the wrong place at the wrong time. Yet a small segment of the world's population realizes that even these events are controlled and influenced by the consciousness of us all. Only those who willingly accept some responsibility for all that happens have any major chance of changing it.

There are those who go through life helplessly and play whatever card life deals them. These people are always a product of their circumstances or their environment. This group of people has surrendered all conscious control over the outcome of their lives to someone or something other than themselves. It's said that if you don't take control over the things that happen in your life that something or someone else will. This group of people accounts for the majority of people out there, and it's this group that is most impressionable to outside influences in their lives. For this reason, it's important that there are people that are there to help direct and influence the thoughts of the masses in a way that benefits both them and society. This is significant since there are people out there doing the opposite. However, remember negative influences can be lessened by the energy we direct toward them via our attitudes, beliefs, thoughts, and opinions.

Your consciousness impacts this last level of creation when you take responsibility for not only your outcomes but even the outcomes caused by others or anything else that's normally not within the apparent control of an individual. The social climate of our society and the attitudes of large groups of people toward the different issues that impact our world can all be influenced by an individual, and that individual could be you. There are only a few people with this level of willingness to accept responsibility for this level of creation and thus attempt to influence it. These are the people who've shaped our world as we know it. A few examples are Gandhi, Martin Luther King Jr., and Mother Teresa. Their attitudes and beliefs have greatly co-created the world that we now know. There are others that have also created experiences that showed us a world that we didn't desire, such as Hitler. I know it's difficult to imagine Hitler's name in the same paragraph as the others mentioned, but he too created on a level that affected everyone globally. He was an example of what most people don't desire, and the others are examples of what most people do. Whether perceived as positive or negative, the most powerful tool that they all used to influence the consciousness of people everywhere was their attitude.

The Power of Belief:

I grew up in a time when it paid off to be tough. But as far back as I can remember, I never wanted to be a bully or a tough guy. As a matter of fact, I despised tough guys. I remember while attending elementary school, in the fifth grade, a school across town, which was considered the rough side of town, burned down to the ground, and all of the students from that school were forced to attend our school. At the time, you couldn't tell me that I didn't run my school; after all, I was popular and had recently been voted the best "whatever" eight out of the ten categories. I was confident that no one could change that. However, what I was not counting on was the fact that the kids that were transferring to my school were not concerned with any of those categories of recognition. They cared more about who the toughest kid was and who the best fighter was. So when this new school joined ours, my focus quickly shifted from being concerned about the things that I felt were important to me, to survival. I had to quickly change my focus from being voted most popular and being most likely to succeed to being the most angered and most likely to survive. This was a very pivotal point in my life because somewhere along the way I made the decision that I was not going to go through my life being bullied, beaten up, or anything that resembled that.

My first real confrontation transpired when a new kid, who was somewhat of a bully, from the other school decided that he liked my girlfriend more than I did and that I should just go away. Naturally, the mere fact that I was in the fifth grade should have ended any thoughts of chivalry or the need to defend what I thought was mine. But my ego (even way back then) kicked in, and there was no way someone was going to come and forcefully take my girlfriend. Actually, the funniest unfunny thing that I remember about this incident is that these young boys were trained in the art of combat to an extent that I knew nothing of. Certainly, I had participated in my fair share of neighborhood brawls and confrontations, but I had never encountered this type of threat before. I remember the young guy who liked my girlfriend telling me that he wanted my girlfriend and that I had better tell her that we were no longer girlfriend and boyfriend so they could be together. As silly as it sounds, I still see adults incorporating the same or similar types of intimidation to acquire what they're after. Anyway, for some reason, his threat didn't phase me (maybe it was love), and I refused to back down, regardless of the troublesome rumors that I had heard about the kids coming from this new school. Besides, until our first confrontation, it was all just gossip. It is amazing, as I look back, just how advanced those kids were to be able to do some of the things that they did. I will never forget walking down the hallway with my childhood sweetheart when three of these kids rushed me and pinned me against a wall with my arms stretched out. As they held me there, a fourth kid (the one that wanted my girlfriend) approached me with about six or seven sharpened pencils tightly gripped in his hand to form a very sharp weapon. He then threatened to stab me in my stomach. As you can imagine, that day had a lasting impression on me. I don't remember why things never went further than they did that day, but I can still feel the same emotions, just as if it were yesterday as I write this. I remember making the decision that I would never allow myself to be victimized again, but I also made the decision that I would never bully anyone else and would defend anyone bullied in my presence. It was that day that shaped the next fifteen years of my life. I dedicated myself to never being bullied, intimidated, or pushed around in any manner.

I remember seeing an interview on *60 Minutes* with Mike Tyson where he was shown video of a few of his early career fights. He told the reporter that at that time he imagined himself as an ancient warrior fighting for his existence and that his mind-set was very damaged at that time and that is what drove him. The reporter then asked him, "Do you think that made you a great fighter?" To which Mike Tyson responded, "I don't know about great, but it definitely made me successful." I instantly related to that comment. I felt the same way about the evolution of my life during those years. Here I was, a guy who got along with pretty much every person that I met. I never met a stranger, and I had hundreds of friends. I was voted most popular every year from elementary school all the way through high school without missing but maybe a year or two. Sounds like a pretty cool guy, doesn't it? Nevertheless, I still somehow found myself in a physical altercation almost on a weekly basis. It was astonishing to most people who knew me then, and those who know me today find it even harder to believe. I wore a suit and carried a briefcase to school every single day of high school. I was always known as the guy with a smile on his face. For that reason, my high school girlfriend constantly told me that she had never met anyone who was loved by so many and hated by just as many at the same time. This was the reason why I found myself fighting constantly. I had somehow convinced myself that I was not going to take anything from anyone for any reason. Furthermore, I possessed the unwavering belief that I wouldn't be beaten regardless of whom I fought or how many people were with them when we fought.

> Your chances of success in any undertaking can always be measured by your belief in yourself.
> —Robert Collier[43]

For those of you who've seen me, you know I'm not the biggest, toughest-looking guy that you're apt to run into, but of the one hundred or more fights that I've fought, I was never hurt, and I never, ever lost. Incredible as this must sound to those reading this, as I write it, it sounds even more unbelievable to me. But I can't explain it any other way other than the fact that my conviction was so strong that where I fell short in physical abilities or skill set, I made up for it in belief and will. I not only maintained the belief that I would win, but I also steadfastly believed that no matter what happened, I would never be hurt, and I never was. Unrealistic enough as it all may sound, add on the fact that at least 70 percent of the fights involved me against more than one person, and I still never lost. I, like Mike Tyson described in that interview, felt like I was under attack at all times; therefore, I was always on guard. I thought about, dreamed about, and planned my reaction to anything that would pop up at any given moment, as it often did. My mind was totally consumed with the thoughts of how to defend against different types of scenarios, so much so that when that time came, my body just flew into an automatic response to whatever was happening. It was almost as if I had played out the scenarios in my mind so many times that when the time came, my body already knew what to do. I now realize that all of the attention I placed on being ready was directly responsible for over 90 percent of the fights that I was in. Most of the people I fought weren't people that I had some personal dealings with where a disagreement had led to a physical altercation. In most cases, these people were complete strangers to me, but for some reason, I would attract these people and situations. These experiences are my earliest conscious awareness of the law of attraction. It wasn't until my friends started to complain that it was dangerous hanging around me that I realized that this was a problem I had better get under control before someone really got hurt, and that's exactly what began to happen. By the time I was a junior or senior in high school, those little groups of kids that I used to fight with had developed into full-blown gangs, and rather than fighting each other, they were now shooting one another. It wasn't until, I changed my belief that everyone who touched me wanted to hurt me and that it was necessary to remain alert at all times because everyone was out to get me that things begin to change. However, this didn't happen until I changed my attitude from negative to positive and stopped focusing on defending myself. Almost overnight, I quit fighting, arguing, or even having disagreements for the most part. As unbelievable as all of this may sound, it's the absolute truth, and this is my strongest personal experience of what is possible with a change in attitude.

Once you have decided what you intend to choose for yourself, have identified the beliefs that support you having it, and have eliminated those beliefs that don't, then you are now ready to proceed to the next truth in your developing life plan. The next truth requires that the first two truths be completely identified before truth number three can be applied. This is crucial because the third truth requires you to set goals to support that which you've decided you want. Obviously, you can't set a goal to do or have something before you identify what it is that you want. Plus, there's no reason to set a goal without a belief system that can support you having it, and this leads us to truth number three.

Truth #3

You must set goals that are in support of what you want.

- Application: After identifying and applying truths number one and two, you must now set goals that are in support of your beliefs and in support of what you now choose to have in your life.

- Explanation: Your goals crystallize your intentions to have what you have now identified you want. By setting goals that are in support of what you want and in support of your beliefs about what you want, you have created the framework for its accomplishment.

- Manifesting Principle: Aligning your goals by creating a roadmap that leads toward their achievement is goal setting in its highest form.

> These truths used together will design your life plan for manifesting:
>
> *Truth #1: The first step to getting what you want is to identify what it is that you want.*
>
> *Truth #2: You must develop beliefs that are in support of your getting what you want.*
>
> *Truth #3: You must set goals that are in support of what you want.*

Once you know what you want, are clear about it, and your beliefs support it, the next logical step is to map out a clear game plan to your goals. The rest happens almost by default. This is the magic behind being an avid goal setter. All goal setters realize that a properly written goal encompasses the two previous truths. This is why people who focus on goal setting as a way of life seem to utilize this manifesting process by default. Each truth can work independently of the truths that preceded it because it encompasses them whether the person using this truth is conscious of it or not. In order to set a goal, you must first begin with the end in mind and decide what you want; thus, you must complete truth number one. Secondly, when a goal is properly set, it gives you clarity, and along with clarity comes belief. Goal setters receive the benefits of the previous truths by default, but when these truths are intentionally used to build your life plan, the process of *manifestation* begins.

The victory of success is half won when one gains the habit of setting goals and achieving them. Even the most tedious chore will become endurable as you parade through each day convinced that every task, no matter how menial or boring, brings you closer to fulfilling your dreams.

—*Og Mandino*[44]

The Power of Goal Setting

There are millions of people who discover every day the power of goal setting. I used to tell people that it doesn't matter if you are someone who lives life by setting goals and going after them or if you are someone who will set a goal just when it's something important. What matters most is that you take the time to set your goals and write them down! In its simplest format, a goal is just a description of something that you want that hopefully also defines when you would like to have it. This, we already know, is the most important part of getting what you want. Consequently, setting a goal requires you to stop and carefully think through what it is that you want. Now, in their highest forms, goals should be more than just a description of something you want. They should be your road map to achieving it.

> The most important thing about goals is having one.
>
> —Geoffry F. Abert[45]

Most people write out their goals and then look back at them a few days or months later and become disenchanted because they rarely accomplish any of the things they set out to do. This is the number one reason people either never set and write out their goals or stop setting them after a few failed attempts. The problem is not the goal setting in and of itself, because that works. The difficulty arises in the type of goal setting that one does. If your goal setting states what you want to accomplish but doesn't provide the smaller steps for the completion of it, then you are bound to miss your mark. For example, if your goal is to lose twenty pounds over the next three months, then what most people simply state is, "My goal is to lose twenty pounds over the next three months." But a properly written goal should also affirm the smaller steps of that goal that ensures its accomplishment. This goal properly written would read like this:

My goal is to lose twenty pounds in ninety days.

- I will accomplish this by walking five miles a day,

- Eating less than 1,800 calories per day,

- And weight training three days a week for a minimum of one hour.

You see, each of the smaller units of your goals is a smaller goal within itself. To walk five miles a day is a goal within itself, and if you accomplish this smaller goal, it will ultimately lead to the accomplishment of the larger goal. This is a simple example of something very powerful. No matter how big the goal is, it will have smaller subaccomplishments that must be met in order to hit your ultimate goal. A goal broken down into these smaller units makes the goal appear less intimidating and more accomplishable. Someone once said that "inch by inch things are a cinch, but yard by yard things are hard." So setting goals and working them through by accomplishing smaller incremental goals allows you to achieve your goals one step at a time.

Happy people plan actions, they don't plan results.

—Denis Waitley[46]

The objective of this chapter is not to train you on how to set goals. Instead it's about making certain that the goals you do set align with and support what you ultimately say you want. There are hundreds of great books and tape series out there that do a more thorough job of breaking down the goal-setting process than what will be attempted here. The type of goal setting outlined in this chapter enlists two requirements in order to manifest your desired results. First, your goals must be set in a way that makes them believable to you. Secondly, your goals must support your life plan.

As I was writing this section of the book, a friend of mine called me and asked me about this exact same subject matter, and our conversation brought tremendous clarity to this subject. He asked the question, "Why is it that sometimes you accomplish the goals that you write out for yourself and sometimes you don't?" And how should he handle the fact that when he rereads his goals from years earlier, he feels disappointment since many of his goals were unaccomplished, which causes him to not want to try again? These questions really made me carefully contemplate the answers, especially since I have faced this dilemma many times. I would go back and reread some of my goals just to realize that I hadn't even attempted many of them. This can be a very frustrating thing. However, I explained to him that a change in approach to goal setting had helped me accomplish almost everything that I truly set my mind to. The first thing I realized upon thinking back on my experiences was that most of the goals I had set had nothing to do with what I really wanted. The next thing I realized was that my goals were not in support of what I wanted, making it clear why I had accomplished so few of them. Thirdly, I noticed that my goals were written out, but I had written nothing in the way of a strategy toward accomplishing them. I now know that you don't need all of the details to set your goals, but the more you do have, the clearer you will become, and the clearer you become, the faster you will manifest what you are after. Lastly, I discovered that I began to live from my goals by making them a part of my lifestyle and that was the principal ingredient. Once I knew what I wanted, became clear about it, aligned my beliefs in support of it, and mapped a clear game plan via my goals toward their accomplishment, the rest happened almost by default. This is the magic behind properly set goals.

> Big goals get big results. No goals get no results or somebody else's results.
>
> —Mark Victor Hansen[47]

The problem with attempting to get something that you want that has yet to be defined with well-written goals is that if you have not determined the way you will go about achieving what you want, then your chances for accomplishing it will be just as undefined. A goal properly set is a goal that not only gives you a date in which you will have your desired results but will also outline the game plan for its accomplishment. Most people avoid setting goals because they're used to the type of goal setting that says, "I will have this or that by this particular date," and then they look up at the end of that described time and wonder why nothing has happened. This haphazard type of goal setting has given one of the most powerful tools in the process of creation a bad rap. The problem is that this is not goal setting but instead it's more like wishful thinking. Most people set these types of so-called goals year after year and never see the achievement of any of them. This type of repeated failure doesn't come from the fact that goal setting doesn't work but rather because a goal that doesn't refine your intentions and provide a step-by-step outline is not a goal that's accomplishable in the first place. Unfortunately, this has been the shared experience of most people. Very few people take the time to formulate, define, and work from well-set goals. Studies show that less than 3 percent of the population consistently sets goals. If this is the case, then I would venture to say that the other 97 percent of the population, at some time or another, has attempted the art of goal setting but did not have the proper training to get it right. This statistic is exactly the same as the fact that 3 percent of the population controls 97 percent of the wealth in the world. Is it possible that one has something to do with the other? I think that they have everything to do with each other, but you will have to be the judge of that. I believe that so many have thrown in the towel on goal setting that in today's society most people go through their lives accomplishing the goals of someone else. Brian Tracy once said, "If you don't set goals for yourself, you are doomed to work to achieve the goals of someone else."[48] This is the threat that all those who intentionally avoid setting goals in fear of the letdown of not achieving them are doomed to live. This is the reason why this truth must be mastered by all who plan to live their lives on their terms, accomplishing the desires of their heart.

A goal properly set is halfway reached.

—Zig Ziglar[49]

How do we proceed to design an effective life plan that will bring about your desired outcomes? The first thing we must do is address the fears associated with setting goals. To do this, we must distinguish between the type of goal setting that has very little chance for success and the type of goal setting that guarantees your success. If the thought of setting goals brings you anxiety, then we must begin to think of goal setting as a step-by-step scientific process rather than a make-a-wish-and-cross-your-fingers kind of a deal. For instance, when you say, "My goal is to be a millionaire by age forty, and I'm now thirty-five years old," and you write this down and do nothing else in support of this, it's the same as closing your eyes and making a wish. You will be no closer on your next birthday when you blow out those candles than you were when there were thirty-two, thirty-three, or thirty-four candles on that cake. However, if your goal says, "I'm thirty-five years old, and my goal is to be a millionaire by my fortieth birthday. I will do this by:

• Doubling my contributions to my 401(k),

• Reducing my spending to increase my savings,

• Eliminating all short-term debt,

• Selling any assets that are not appreciating,

• Reinvesting this money into appreciating assets.

• Investing 35 percent of my income in investments that will yield a minimum return of 20 percent annually.

"Based on the amount of money I have saved, the amount of money I have accumulated in my 401(k), and by investing 35 percent of my income for the next five years at a rate of return of 20 percent annually, I will have raised a sum of one million dollars."

Does this sound like a wish or a game plan? With that in mind, if you wrote down a goal and then had a goal-setting expert take you through the process of breaking down that goal into smaller, logical steps that produced a road map like the previous example, do you still think you would have a fear of setting goals?

> Make no little plans they have no magic to stir men's blood, and probably themselves will not be realized. Aim high in hope and work, remembering that a noble, logical diagram once recorded will not die.
>
> —Daniel H. Burnham[50]

The second thing we must do is learn to work from our goals versus toward them. To do this, you must set goals that are big enough to make you stretch but still attainable enough to create the excitement and enthusiasm necessary to achieve anything worth striving for. If your goals don't excite you, you should set new ones. This will give you the motivation it takes to complete each task no matter how small. When goals are properly set and written in a way that outlines how they will be accomplished, every seeming failure will be viewed as feedback versus a setback. In this way, your goals should focus on the achievement of the smaller goals and not just on the end result.

Two of the more common mistakes made when it comes to setting goals are making your goals too far-fetched or too realistic. Both of these scenarios will result in you missing your mark. The problem with setting goals that are too lofty is that you won't believe in them, and if you don't believe in your goals, you aren't going to take the actions to go for it. However, the problem with setting them too realistically is that you will often lower your expectations, and you won't have the motivation to pursue them. While setting realistic goals may seem like a logical thing to do, in reality, it can leave you totally uninspired and feeling unmotivated about your goals. Most people will set realistic goals, such as, "I will cover my cost for my new business and be profitable in the first two years." This sounds like a good goal, but on tough days, do you see this goal giving you the excitement that will have you jumping out of bed in the morning and staying up late at night to accomplish it? What if that same goal was, "I will cover all of my costs, get out of debt, and make a million dollars in my first year of business?" Do you think this goal could keep you inspired during the tough times? Of course, if you are in an industry that doesn't have this type of upside, then obviously you will need to make adjustments, but if anyone else in your industry has ever had that level of success, then so can you. The very fact that someone else has accomplished it should make it doable for you. You need to set goals that are beyond your reach and large enough to really get your juices flowing. Then when you think about your new, bigger goals, you'll get excited just imagining what it would feel like to reach them and what your life will be like having accomplished them. If you make your goals a little more than what you're already getting, then you won't need to imagine what that would feel like because you already know. Do you see how this can take some of the enthusiasm out of your plans? Even if you don't fully reach your bigger goal, you'll still go way beyond what you might have accomplished with a realistic goal.

To be able to work from your goals versus toward your goals, you must first ask yourself these questions: are my goals exciting, and are my goals refined enough to be realistic, but far reaching enough to be inspiring? There's nothing more handicapping than a goal that is written below what you know you can achieve. So if your current goals don't excite you, then you should stop here and rewrite them. Any goal that you have that don't excite you should be moved to your to-do list and should not make it to your goal list. A goal is a target. That target should obviously be visible, but it still should be well beyond your immediate grasp. If not, then either set a new goal or redefine the ones that you have.

If you have done the exercises in the chapter for truth number one and decided what you truly want, then you should already be excited because that should be your goal. Now all that's left to do is to properly set it. After you know what you desire, which you will list as your goal, and you have the proper attitude about it, it's time to work backward and outline all the necessary steps that you will need to take in order to make it happen. The first step is you need to make a list of everything that you can think of that needs to happen in order for this goal to be realized. If your goal includes purchasing a building or office equipment or finding the right employees or partners, you should put that on your list. If you know that you're going to need a Web site and an advertising firm, they should also be included on this list. The second step is to place those items in the order in which they will need to be completed in the grand scheme of your ultimate goal. Remember, the more details you can add to this plan, the more realistic your goals will appear, and the more realistic they are, the more believable they will become. Once all of the smaller steps are outlined, take each of those smaller steps and check them to see if they have even smaller substeps that create a road map for the larger step's accomplishment. Upon completion of this process, review it as often as possible and write in any new details as they come up during the process. After every known step and substep has been identified, it's now time to develop the timeline for when these things should be accomplished. You will again begin with the end in mind and work backward, so decide on the date that you would like to see this goal accomplished. Begin to set the smaller dates that outline the amount of time it will take to hit the smaller steps and do the same with your subgoals. Doing this may cause you to rework your dates a few times until the dates all add up to a challenging but obtainable timeline. Don't get discouraged if the date that you originally thought of and the date that you end up with are far apart from each other. Remember, this plan is designed to help you achieve your goals, not merely establish that you have one. Everything that provides more clarity enhances your belief in your goal, your plan to accomplish it, and the knowledge that you are prepared to achieve it. Each of the smaller steps is a goal in and of itself and so are the substeps. Bear in mind, if you don't hit your smaller goals, then don't be surprised when the larger goals are missed as well. Before you move to the final step, remember to notify anyone you need to participate in this process of his or her involvement and the timelines. Once your properly set goal is checked and rechecked, write or type it out. It's now time for the final step and that's to take this clearly defined plan and break down each goal into daily or weekly activities. Each plan should list the activity that must be accomplished that day or week so that you can stay on target with the outlined schedule. As each item is completed, come back and scratch it off your master list and your daily or weekly activity plan.

> Decide...whether or not the goal is worth the risks involved. If it is, stop worrying...Worry retards reaction and makes clear-cut decisions impossible.
>
> —Amelia Earhart[51]

Thomas Edison, the inventor of the light bulb and "the first genuinely safe and economically viable system for generating and distributing light and power worldwide" was quoted as saying, "If I find ten thousand ways something won't work, I haven't failed. I am not discouraged, because every wrong attempt discarded is often a step forward." [52] [53] Take this same attitude as you work your daily activity plan, understanding that each result, whether positive or negative, will get you that much closer to hitting your mark. When working from your goals versus toward your goals, you are forced to work backward, beginning with the end in mind. This gives you the opportunity to see the end result and allows you to experience being there mentally first. This is where everything that now exists in our physical world originates: in the minds of men and women.

I taught goal-setting workshops while I was a part of a network marketing company, and I used much of what I'm referencing here, but when I wrote this book, it took every step of the before-mentioned goal-setting exercise for me to manifest its completion. It started with making the decision to truly do it and set a completion date. I made this decision in 2002, but it wasn't until June of 2004 that I even began writing the first line of this book with the completion date of June 2006.

A clear vision, backed by definite plans, gives you a tremendous feeling of confidence and personal power.

—Brian Tracy[54]

When I began writing this book, I was dealing with the many distractions of my very busy lifestyle. At the time, I had six companies, all of which required my active involvement. So the process was slow, and before I knew it, another two years had gone by, and very little had been written. As I reviewed the bits and pieces that I had written, I instantly knew that I needed to seriously revisit this goal-setting exercise. Once I went through the process and set my new goal of completing this book by June of 2008, outlined in the way being described, I realized that I had not even started.

Therefore, if I had any chance of getting this project completed, it would require me to follow this exercise to a tee. So I began with the end in mind and decided what I wanted to get accomplished and when I wanted to complete it. I then set the smaller goals and included the dates each task would need to be finished in order to hit the larger goals. As I went through this process, I began to set even smaller goals for when various aspects of this book and the program would need to be completed. I then chose the tasks that I would need to work on first and which tasks made sense to do last and attached dates to those things as well. This process forced me to change my completion date many, many times, as my vision continued to expand and my game plan became more structured and clear. My friends and family began saying, "Why don't you send us some of what is already complete," but I didn't have much to send. This was proof enough that setting my goals in a way that would ensure their accomplishment was an absolute must. As soon as I finally got my plan together and developed my daily activity schedule, things really picked up and started to happen. I began remembering stories that I had read and television programs that I had watched that related to what was being written, and this process began to take on a life of its own. It started to feel as though I wasn't writing as much as I was taking dictation from someone else who was doing the writing of this book. It was at this point that I realized that I was using the seven truths, and what Patanjali had described 2,300 years ago was now coming to pass in the writing of this book and the developing of the other aspects of the accompanying program. If you have ever had this type of experience, then you were probably aware that it was happening, and if you haven't, then use these Sutra's as your guide.

When you are inspired by some great purpose,
some extraordinary project
All of your thoughts break their bonds,
Your mind transcends limitations,
Your consciousness expands in every direction.

You find yourself in a new and a great and a wonderful world.
Dormant forces, facilities and talents come alive.
You discover yourself to be a greater person by far
than you ever dreamed yourself to be.
—Patanjali[55]

Everything seemed to be working at warp speed, and I somehow
had all the tools at my disposal for the completion of the writing of
this book. All types of synchronistic things began to happen. People
began calling and asking me to host conference calls to explain the
seven truths and upload my information on Web sites. As I became
more engrossed in this process, more and more people began to ask
what it was that I was working on, and as I told them, they began
to ask me if they could book me for seminars. Prior to working this
goal-setting exercise, few of these things were happening. As I mar-
veled at this process unfolding in front of my eyes, one of the synchronistic events that transpired was I came across some notes that I
had written out of a book I had read several years earlier. The notes
were from a book called *The Seven Habits of Highly Effective People*
by Steven Covey. As I read through the notes, some of what was
being described fit perfectly with this chapter, but as I got to the
part where I had written out each of the seven habits, I immediately
knew the real reason why this information was put back in front of
me. As you read the seven habits below and the notes that accom-
pany them that these highly effective people possess, see if you find
the same similarities that I found when I compared them to *The 7
Truths of Life*. When I read these, I was blown away.

The 7 Habits of Highly Effective People [56]

• The First habit is: Be Proactive–Principles of Personal Vision
(Which means take responsibility for you own life–Responsibility–the ability to choose your own response–*Truth #1*)

• The Second habit is: Begin with the End in Mind–Principles of

Personal Leadership(There are always two creations—the mental creation and the physical creation—*Truths #1, 3, and 4)*

- The Third habit is: Put First Things First—Principles of Personal Management (The key is to not manage time, but manage yourself—*Truth #2 & 3)*

- The Fourth habit is: Think Win/Win—Principles of Interpersonal Leadership (The attitude of seeking solutions so that everyone can win—*Truths 2 & 4)*

- The Fifth habit is: Seek First to Understand, Then to Be Understood Principles of Empathic Communication (Communicate by listening first then responding—*Truth # 5)*

- The Sixth habit is: Synergize—Principles of Creative Cooperation (The habit of Creative Corporation—*Truth #6)*

- The Seventh habit is: Sharpen the Saw—Principles of Balanced Self-Renewal (The habit of self-renewal—The self-maintenance habit—*Truth # 7)*

All who have accomplished great things have had a great aim; have fixed their gaze on a goal which was high, one which sometimes seemed impossible.
—Orison Swett Marden[57]

As I completed writing this goal-setting chapter, I realized that I had never explained nor had this goal-setting process explained to me in more simpler or clearer terms. It made me contemplate who was actually doing the writing here, and I instantly became in awe of these seven truths and their implications. Setting your goals in this way will totally consume you and will launch you on your way to what you are after. Therefore, this goal-setting truth is important because it insures that you use the two truths that precede it by default, and it sets up the proper usage of the remaining truths. When this goal-setting process is complete, you will be prepared to choose the right thoughts, words, and actions that have already been outlined in your well-written game plan.

Truth #4

You must think thoughts that
are in support of what you want.

- Application: You must intentionally choose thoughts that support what you have decided that you want, the beliefs that you have, and the goals that you have set.

- Explanation: Your thoughts are things, and what you think about is what will come about. Intentionally putting thoughts together that support what you want creates and manifests into your reality exactly what your prechosen thoughts are.

- Manifesting Principle: You must visualize in your mind that which you desire to manifest into your reality.

  These truths used together will design your life plan for manifesting:

  Truth #1: The first step to getting what you want is to identify what it is that you want.

  Truth #2: You must develop beliefs that are in support of your getting what you want.

  Truth #3: You must set goals that are in support of what you want.

Truth #4: You must think thoughts that are in support of what you want.

Applying what's being taught requires that you look at what is starting to formulate as you continue to refine your life plan. Most people who have discovered the process of creation, through someone else or figured it out for themselves, usually all begin the lesson here at truth number four and then proceed forward. But as you can see, purposeful thinking is determined by beginning with the end in mind and deciding upfront that which you choose to have show up in your life. Once this has been accomplished, to ensure that the right thoughts are selected, you must then make certain that your beliefs are in support of what you are choosing. If not, you will have the first truth correct, but you will never manifest your desires because your beliefs about it will send you in the wrong direction. This is why correct beliefs precede correct thoughts, but correct thoughts receive their marching orders from a clearly defined, well-thought-out game plan. With truth number one, two, and three properly aligned, the next logical step in this evolutionary process of creation is to purposefully design thoughts that support your life plan.

As a man thinketh in his heart so does he become.

Proverbs 23:7[58]

Think About What You Think About

Do you ever think about what you think about? If the answer is no, then this will soon change after you discover the relationship between your thoughts and the things that show up in your life every day. This process has been explained by every enlightened teacher that has ever walked this earth. It is a pretty established fact that what you think about, you will talk about; what you talk about, you will act upon; and what you act upon repeatedly becomes a habit. Your habits determine your character, and your character is who you are. So only think of what you do want and never think about that which you don't, for what you think about is what will come about. If you find yourself not totally satisfied with who and what you are, then you must begin the process of thinking a new thought about it. For this reason, you must teach yourself to think thoughts that are in alignment with what you choose for yourself, or it will never come about. Most people think about the exact opposite. They dwell on what's missing in their lives that they would like to have show up, and all they continue to get is more of what's missing. For this reason, you must guard your thoughts, for thoughts are energy, and the thoughts you have will eventually manifest themselves in your life.

Whatsoever the mind dwells upon it must become!

—Gertrude A. Bradford[59]

The highest form of thinking is to visualize in your mind that which you wish to show up in your reality. This is what is meant by the saying, "Where there is no vision the people perish" (Proverbs 29:18).[60] In order to accomplish anything in your life, you must first hold a vision of it in your mind. The mind works in pictures, not words. Words are powerful, but remember, a picture is worth a thousand words. It's for this reason that the tool of visualization is the manifesting principle of this truth.

Perhaps this is a good time to further define what is meant by manifesting something versus creating it. The verb for turning thoughts into form is to manifest. It comes from the world of imagination and the Middle English word *manifestus,* meaning visible, and the Latin word *manus,* meaning hand.[61] When you manifest something, you metaphorically reach your hand through the invisible curtain, separating the tangible world, and pull your desired object into existence.[62] Have you ever thought of someone and he or she called or thought of someone you haven't seen in a long time and you ran into him or her the same day? What most people write off as a coincidence or a fluke is really the answer to a request from the subconscious mind. I remember once talking with an old friend on the phone, and he asked me when was the last time I had spoken with a particular person, someone that I hadn't spoken with in over ten years. We talked about him for several minutes and as we ended the conversation I remember saying how much I would love to talk to that person, and how I wish I knew how to get in touch with him. We disconnected the call, and the second I hung up, my cell phone vibrated, letting me know that I had a new message. I checked the voice mail, and it was my friend that I hadn't spoken with in ten years saying hello and leaving me his contact information. Even the most skeptical person would have to agree that this was more than just a coincidence. Or maybe this was a coincidence but one based on the mathematical definition, for the word *coincidence* comes from coincide, and mathematically, when two angles coincide, they fit together perfectly.

In this era of our scientific research, almost no one debates the power of the mind.

I once watched a documentary on the power of the mind and how the very thought of a thing could impact every aspect of your being; everything from your mental, physical, spiritual, and emotional being is affected by the power of suggestion that comes from your thoughts. It's a well-known fact that your conscious mind stands as the guard to your subconscious mind. This makes what you program into your conscious mind very important because it filters what the almighty subconscious mind gets access to. The filter that the conscious mind uses to decide what makes it through to your subconscious is your belief system. Those thoughts that coincide with your current set of beliefs, once checked against your registry of experiences, beliefs, and general attitude, make it through without refining. Those thoughts that are similar but not quite the same as your dominating thoughts are checked, possibly refined, and then passed through and adopted. Your thoughts sort of stay in limbo until other information comes through that either supports them or rejects them. It is this entire filtering process that is bypassed when someone is hypnotized, or if he or she suffers from multiple personality disorders. Did you know that in both cases when a thought gets past the conscious mind and gets directly to the subconscious, it is automatically believed and is made true in that person's reality? Thus, when someone is told that he or she has a cold while hypnotized, they will not only start to feel like he or she thinks they should feel when sick with a cold but they also get the physical symptoms as well. From coughing, fever, to a runny nose, all these physical symptoms show up within seconds of this thought being planted on the subconscious mind. You can take a truly sick person whose body is filled with cancer, and if that same person suffers from multiple personalities, switch to a personality of a cancer-free person, test him or her within minutes and he or she will be 100 percent cancer free. Amazingly, this has been proven in thousands of cases, whether it's someone suffering from a multiple personality disorder or someone under the care of a hypnotist such phenomenon happen.[63]

> Thought backed by strong desire has a tendency to transmute itself into its physical equivalent.
>
> —Napoleon Hill[64]

Now, what does this tell you about your mind? If your conscious mind decides what makes it to your subconscious mind, then we must make certain that our conscious mind sends the right message to our subconscious since, as this example demonstrates, the subconscious is going to bring about whatever is pressed on to it. Hence, your thoughts are your direct link to your subconscious mind. Your thoughts are the most powerful tools you have to pass on messages to your subconscious. That's why it is said that if you don't like the results you are getting, then change your mind about it. In order to change your mind about the things it currently allows to pass through this filtering process, you have to reprogram the conscious mind to accept the things you desire and reject the things that are bringing undesired results. Intentionally choosing the same preselected thoughts through visualization is the quickest way to make this happen. If you take the time to create a picture, whether physical or in your mind, of what you would like to have show up in your life, things will start to happen that will catapult you toward the vision you hold.

This is where this phenomenon of creating picture boards sprung from. People would find pictures that represented what they wanted, put them on a visualization board, and place it somewhere it could be viewed often. Over time, these people would realize they had attracted many of the pictures on the board into their actual reality. I wasn't a big fan of this process until I started watching Oprah. Now, before you start to jump to any conclusions, it was my wife watching Oprah, I was just in the room (at least this is the excuse that I use). This seems to be the only time that I can get my wife to sit still long enough to pamper me (massage me). In fact, I can ask her to do anything during this time as long as it doesn't require her to take her eyes off the television. And it always works like a charm. So as I laid there listening, getting my usual daily, schemed-upon massage, I started telling my wife before the guest would come on to watch for the guest to say that they always envisioned themselves sitting there talking with Oprah, or they would say that they had put a picture of Oprah on their picture board and had dreamed of one day sitting there with her. And sure enough, one by one they would say it, and there they were sitting there with Oprah regardless of how strange the set of circumstances were that landed them there.

> Imagination will often carry us to worlds that never were. But without it we go nowhere.
>
> —Carl Sagan[65]

I was now beating my wife to the television when it was Oprah time to hear the next story; besides that, Oprah was good! As I watched guest after guest, the most common thing that I heard was that they were creating picture boards, and they would put something representing the show on their board. I said to myself, "Boy, I need to start making some picture boards. I had done this once or twice before by placing the pictures in a room where I use to write and meditate. It was hidden in the back of my master bath's closet. It was a nice-sized room that I had covered the better part of the ceiling with various pictures, quotes, and sayings that inspired me. This didn't work too well since at the time I changed my mind pretty frequently about the things that I wanted. So I would either have to find new pictures or look at the things that I no longer wanted. Finally, I decided it was best to hold a mental image in my mind of whatever it was that I sought. This worked better for me because I could change this mental picture as often as I liked, and I could make any adjustment to that image that I wanted to, unlike a picture out of a magazine. I would encourage you to do the same. You also can add feelings to your visualization, unlike looking at a picture. This is a very important aspect of your mental movie because emotions determine the speed in which the impressions hit your subconscious mind. The more excited you are about the visualization that you create, the faster your subconscious will recognize it as your command, just like a genie in a bottle. This is where your imagination comes into play. Your imagination adds fuel to the fire of your visualization. You see, your visualization often only allows you to see in your mind what is currently so, but your imagination is what allows you to see what you would like for it to be. Imagination is one of the most powerful tools of creation. It manifests things into being with the emotions and excitement that come from you seeing the things you want in your future in their fullest versions before they actually are. Mozart once said that the symphonies that he created presented themselves to him in what he called "lively dreams." He was nine years old.[66] It was his imagination at work as the process of creation presented itself to him in these dreams. Albert Einstein once said, "Imagination is more important than knowledge."[67] And Vincent Van Gogh said, "I dream my painting and then paint my dream."[68] These are just a few examples of people who mastered the use of this very powerful tool.

There is a law in psychology that if you form a picture in your mind of what you would like to be, and you keep and hold that picture there long enough, you will soon become exactly as you have been thinking.

—William James[69]

Seeing What You Want

What does what you want look like? Be creative and as detailed as you possibly can and determine what will go into the creation of this mini movie in your mind that plays out precisely your desired results. I remember watching Michael Jordan being interviewed about his pregame routine, and he told the interviewer that he plays out the entire game in his mind, and he sees it ending the way he wants the game to end. So I began trying this right before I would go on stage for a speaking or training event. I would visualize the audience receiving the information and getting out of it what I intended to relay to them. I would watch myself deliver a confident, brilliant speech or training and watch the audience respond to my comments. I would go as far as seeing people laughing when I told jokes, becoming serious when the subject matter changed, and even crying if I had planned to tell a story that would stir that type of emotion. As silly as this may sound, I would often see the exact reaction at different times during my training that I had envisioned. The first few times this happened, it startled me so much that I had to pause to find my place.

Everyone has, at some time or another, experienced seeing something in his or her mind and then have seen it play out right in front of their eyes or have had a song flash across his or her mind and turned on the radio and that song was playing. This is not by chance, and it's no accident. You should begin paying attention to the times that this happens and document the circumstances surrounding it. The more you do this, the more you will notice it occurring, just like when you bought that car that no one else had and you begin to see them everywhere. The messages will become clearer, and the more you look for these clues that are sent there to direct you and help guide you along the way, the more they will show up, and the more they show up, the more you will recognize them and actually learn to trust and depend on them. You will become one who always looks and listens for messages of synchronicity. When you remember how this works, you realize that it's all being driven by the thoughts that are making it through the filters of your conscious mind to your subconscious. I now rely so heavily on this process that even when I'm not in sync and I'm not paying attention, my subconscious continues to send messages until I eventually realize that this is what's happening again.

There was a time I was so distraught with my current set of circumstances that I felt it had become very difficult to do what normally came very naturally to me. From this experience I eventually realized that sometimes when you get so far removed that you begin to feel disconnected, your subconscious has to jolt you back into alignment with the guiding force of your purpose. I remember feeling so out of balance that I felt awkward, as if I were somehow out of sync. It was a feeling I hadn't had in a long time since the business I was in required me to be at the top of my game at all times. It was like not being able to find my rhythm. It was the opposite of being in that zone where things normally just seem to flow and only go in the direction of your desire. At this time, I couldn't get anything right. I remember praying and meditating about getting my life back on track. I constantly had the feeling that I was moving farther and farther away from my purpose. That was the only explanation that made sense while I tried to find my way back. The company I was involved in afforded me the opportunity to do presentations and training several times a week. This continued practice at public speaking helped me to become a pretty good speaker, and I excelled greatly in that regard. But at this particular time, I couldn't seem to present the information with ease as I had done so often. One event in particular that I was scheduled to do was an all day presentation in Chattanooga, Tennessee, which I somehow knew would be a challenge for me. I was accustomed to leading training sessions for six to eight hours straight without the use of notes or visual aids because I knew the material so well. However, this Saturday morning, I was looking for every aid I could find. I had planned to show videos and anything else I could get my hands on. Just as I suspected, I struggled through the first part of the presentation that I had done hundreds of times. Once that was over and before the training began, I went to my car and sat there with my eyes closed, meditating and con-templating what was going wrong that was causing me to struggle so badly and what it would take to get back on track. I went back in for the second half and did my best and finished out that day. As my wife and I drove home that evening, she asked me what was wrong and why I looked so uncomfortable during the seminar. I explained to her what I'd been going through for the past month or two and that I felt it was getting worse. Just as we finished the conversation, a good friend of mine gave me a call and asked if my wife and I would like to come over for dinner and a movie. This was exactly what I needed, considering the day I had just had. He also told me that the movie he wanted us to watch was a must see and that he felt that I would get a lot out of it. So we went for dinner but ended up talking the entire night and never had a chance to watch the movie. He told me the name of the movie was *The Legend of Bagger Vance*, which was a movie about golf, so I wasn't very excited. Still, he insisted that I take the movie home and watch it that evening. I went home that night, left the movie on my entertainment system, and went straight to bed. The following morning, I was lying in bed, and my wife woke me up to tell me that one of my favorite authors, Dr. Wayne Dyer, was on PBS speaking before an audience. I woke up just enough to lie there and listen. Just as I tuned in, Dr. Dyer began to tell a story that had happened several years earlier during the time this program was originally recorded. The first thing that caught my attention was that he said, "Yesterday, I was in Chattanooga, Tennessee, doing a talk for a group of people."[70] My wife immediately looked at me and said, "Yesterday, we were in Chattanooga, Tennessee, and you were doing a presentation." As I sat up in the bed, I told my wife, "Wow, that's really weird." The next thing he said immediately got us both to our feet. He proceeded to say that after his speech a friend called and asked him if he would like to come by for dinner, just as my friend had asked me the night before, and that at dinner he gave him a book that he wanted to share with him called *The Legend of Bagger Vance*.[71] As you can imagine, my wife and I were floored, and we both ran into the living room to grab the movie and turn it on. I knew that the universe was trying to tell me something, and I had to view this movie to get to the bottom of what it was. When I got the message of the movie, I instantly knew that I was not going through this thing called life alone and that there was an order and a sense of perfection that existed in the entire universe and this perfection governed my life. The movie was about a golfer and his caddy. And the golfer was being taught by his caddy how to get his swing back. The movie is based on a book written by Steven Pressfield entitled *The Legend of Bagger Vance: Golf and the Game of Life*. At the time, I didn't know what the subtitle of the book was because I would have immediately known that this was the universe's way of answering my question of how to get my swing back. When I first heard Dr. Dyer name the book, I didn't wait to hear anything else. Naturally, since it was a movie, I had to sit and watch the entire film to learn that there were these four pathways to mastery being taught that I needed to learn. In this movie, Bagger Vance is a caddy, played by Will Smith, who is teaching Junuh, the golfer, played by Matt Damon, how to get his swing back.[72] This was the perfect message for me at that time, and it helped me to get my life back on track. The four under-lining tools that Bagger Vance taught Junuh in this film were that when pursuing anything, there are four pathways to master:[73]

1. Discipline

2. Wisdom

3. Unconditional Love

4. Surrender

I immediately took heed to the message that the universe had just shared with me through this movie and was left in awe by the method that was used to communicate the answer to my question.

The Challenge

If the mind is left alone to freely think anything it wishes, it will follow the dominant thought pattern of the person, and this is where most people experience the real challenge. If you are typically a person who thinks about the problem (even if you are trying to think of the solution), you will typically think about what you are worried about; therefore, you manifest more of what you are worried about. And this cycle continues. You think about the problem and that helps to create more of the problem, thus giving you more of that problem to think about. On the other hand, if you think about your dreams and the things that you want, then the same is true. You bring about what you think about. Therefore, if your focus is on the things that you want and not on the things that you don't want, you will think thoughts that are in harmony with what you seek. Even thinking positively about what you don't want will only bring about more of what you don't want. People who say things like, "Well, we will just make the best of it" or "It could have been worse" are trying to think positively about something that they didn't want. Or the person who puts all of his or her efforts and energy into not being hurt again in a relationship always seems to attract the type of person who will help bring about the very results he or she is trying to avoid. It's the difference between the person who says, "I will never be hurt by another person in a relationship again" versus the person who says, "I will only attract the type of person who will love and respect me and be my perfect mate." Do you see the difference? One statement simply says what is desired and the other states what's desired by saying what's not. In both cases, the person always gets what he or she focuses his or her attention upon.

> It's not what you are that holds you back; it's what you think you
> are not.
>
> —Denis Waitley[74]

To take control of your thoughts and make certain that they support your goals, your beliefs, and your desires, you must first understand which thoughts of yours focus on what you want, which ones do not, and how to differentiate between the two. To do this, we will need to explore how we attract thoughts, how the ones selected affect us, and how to rid ourselves of the ones that don't support us.

The Three Types of Thoughts

There are three types of thoughts: those that originate from you, thoughts that originate from someone else, and the body of thoughts that have belonged to everyone everywhere since the beginning of time. This body can be referred to as the collective consciousness. Every thought that you have and ever had lives alongside every thought anyone else has ever had. Most of the thoughts that we think originate from us are actually pulled from this shared pool of thoughts that already exist within the collective consciousness. That's why you can't turn your thoughts off; they move across your mind like pictures on a movie screen. You then select which thoughts from this continuous stream you will call your own. Of the infinite number of thoughts that have existed since the beginning of time, you draw to you daily the thousands that will flash through your mind. These thoughts are drawn to you by your attitude and typically are in alignment with your beliefs. This belief-attitude relationship was explained in chapter two, and it is essential that this process be understood since it directly impacts the thought process. This is the reason truth number two precedes this one because it dictates 100 percent of the thoughts that you will have to select from. The thoughts that you select from this collective consciousness determine what transpires in your universe and thus shapes the entire universe. This is the meaning behind the common adage, "The first step to changing the world is to change your world." Most people teach that creation starts here, for this is the most powerful tool that we have access to. When you attract thoughts that are the highest representations of you and choose to think them, you are also choosing the highest thoughts out of the body of thoughts retained within our collective consciousness. Your highest thoughts will not only serve you, but thinking it also serves this body. You will know these thoughts because they will bring you feelings of joy, enthusiasm, love, and peace. If you continue to choose these types of thoughts, then more of these positive thoughts will be attracted to you, and you will have even more thoughts to choose from to multiply those feelings. Consequently, this is good for the collective consciousness because when the majority of your thoughts bring you joy and happiness versus anger and fear, it not only impacts you but all those around you and all of those that are in alignment with that type of thinking. The more you draw thoughts of joy and happiness to yourself, the more others in contact with you will begin to have these same or similar thoughts to choose from. If this cycle continues long enough, it will begin to shape the collective consciousness itself, resulting in a shift in consciousness. Of course, the exact opposite is true. The more people who attract and think fear-based thoughts, the more that consciousness expands as well. In this way, each of us has the ability to drastically impact all of us.

You may be asking yourself, "How am I supposed to select a thought that will bring me the feeling of fulfillment when I'm living in a situation that's opposite of what I desire?" This can be fixed more easily than you think. Every human on the planet has a naturally built-in instinct to avoid pain and seek pleasure. As you began your mental diet, start to choose thoughts that bring you pleasurable feelings versus thoughts that arouse feelings of pain. This is an easy process. Every time you have a thought and you are determining if you will keep that thought, focus on how it makes you feel and ask yourself, "Does this thought bring me more pain or more pleasure?" If the answer is more pain, then simply choose another thought. Continue this process and you will begin to see that more often than not, all the thoughts you have to choose between are thoughts that bring you pleasure. This is when you will begin to move from only self-serving thoughts to thoughts that serve your higher self, which will also serve humanity as a whole. The quickest way to get to the thoughts that serve the higher you is to satisfy the lower you and get that out of the way. Find one humanitarian or anyone else that uses his time, talents, and resources to serve the world and look and see if his personal desires have already been met or not. Ten times out of ten, these are people who have already found their personal fulfillment. That is the reason why the message and application of the truths in this book are so important. As you find your purpose and begin to fulfill the desires of your heart, others will be attracted to your success. As you help them discover and live their passions, fewer and fewer people will suffer from the lower thought processes. They will start to attract higher thoughts just from being in association with you, and thoughts such as fear, doubt, and scarcity will begin to fade away. This is very significant because fearful and doubtful thinking pushes you further away from what you desire. If the thought processes of the people you spend the most time with are self-defeating or center on lack, then you may have to remove them from your circle while on this mental diet. In essence, birds of the same feather really do flock together, both literally and metaphorically. You are the company you keep, and you tend to share the same types of thoughts that this company thinks. It is for this reason that it is very difficult to escape the gravitational pull of the group consciousness that you belong to. This may seem like a very difficult thing to do, considering there is a good chance that you will be surrounded by people who think in terms of scarcity or lack of abundance. However, if you continue to think the way they think, you will continue to get what they have. Through this material, you will attain the understanding that we live in a perfect universe where there is no lack, for whatever is missing, your desires to have it will create it in enough abundance that whether ten, ten thousand, or ten million people desire the same thing, the universe is beyond capable of manifesting the exact amount summoned. This knowledge allows you to shift from selecting thoughts of lack, jealousy, and envy to abundance, contentment, and appreciation.

If you don't like something change it; if you can't change it, change
the way you think about it.

—Mary Engelbreit[75]

As you begin to realize your desires, do you see how you will no longer have any need to desire something of someone else's or be envi-
ous when you either have or know how to get what you seek? This
change in individual consciousness impacts the group consciousness
that you belong to and the consciousness of all people everywhere.
Nevertheless, before you can develop it, you may have to separate
yourself from the group consciousness that you now belong to. You
must do this until you develop your individual consciousness to the
point that it can impact the groups rather than being impacted by
the group. If not, you will always be a product of the consciousness of
the group of people that you spend the most time with. Your second
option is to find a group whose consciousness is in sync with where
you would like for yours to go and let their influence impact your
consciousness, in this case for the better. Despite the way you decide
to get there; it's your responsibility to make it happen.

This shift in consciousness you will make is instrumental to
returning our world back to its natural balance and will eventually alleviate all crime, disease, and unwanted natural calamities. As
unrealistic as this may sound and fairy tale like, there are civiliza-
tions on our planet that are currently experiencing the benefits of
the natural state described here. In his book *Power vs. Force*, David
Hawkins suggests that:

> Objectively, it can be seen that thoughts really belong to the con-
> sciousness of the world; the individual mind merely processes
> them in new combinations and permutations. What are seen to be
> truly original thoughts appear only through the medium of genius
> and are invariably felt by their authors to be a gift, found or given;
> not self-created. It may be the case that we're each unique, as no
> two snowflakes are alike ... however, we're still just snowflakes.[76]

For there is nothing either good or bad, but thinking makes it so.

—William Shakespeare[77]

I knew theoretically that what you think about consistently creates on one level and, if contemplated long enough, will come to pass, but I didn't know experientially until later in my life. I discovered that your subconscious mind does not know the difference between good and bad, happy and sad, or right and wrong. So whether your intentions are what you consider good or bad, make certain that your thoughts about it are consistent with your desired outcome. I thought that I had mastered this concept, and I often told people during my seminars that if you are going to rob banks and do other bad things of that nature, then I wouldn't suggest hanging out with people who are afraid of guns and who are nonconfrontational. And then I would tell them that if they enjoyed a peaceful, nonviolent lifestyle, then they might not want to hang with the bank-robbing group. In other words, you have to select the people you want to spend your time with purposefully to make certain that they are heading in the same direction that you are heading. And I would go on and on about the company you keep and how people that spend a lot time together do so because they think alike and that is the strongest attraction that brings people together. So I could always tell the types of thoughts people chose for themselves by the company they kept.

For the most part, I was convinced of this, but I didn't know it to be undeniably true until I did a meditation once called Japa, which I learned from a tape series taught by Dr. Wayne Dyer.[78] This mediation allows you to manifest anything you want in your life just by focusing your attention on it and doing this meditation once in the morning and again in the evening. During this meditation, you focus on what you intend to create in your life while repeating the sound of creation. This sound, by the way, can be discovered by looking at every major religion in the world and sounding out the name that they use for God and looking for the sound that's common in every name, just in case you want to try this for yourself. Also, you are instructed to repeat a different sound in the evening, the sound of all things created, remembering that for everything that exists, its sound is measured in ohms.[79]

I did this every morning and every evening with a good friend who I've traveled this path toward enlightenment with. We would call each other, place our phones on speaker, and do this meditation, both individually focusing on what we intended to create, and then after about ten minutes, we would pick the phone up and just talk about whatever was on our minds at the time. One of the consistent conversations that we had was about his wife and their kids and the different things that were happening with them, and I would counter with what little conversation that I could, considering at the time I wasn't married or seriously dating anyone. During this period, I was in one of my lower states when it came to male-female relationships. I've since that time realized this, but at the time I thought that things couldn't have been better. I was having the time of my life dating whomever I wished whenever I wished. Nevertheless, since we were on the subject of wives and kids, I would often limit my conversation to my fantasy of the ideal person for me and the ideal circumstances required for me to settle down and marry. Sometimes we would talk for over an hour, at which time I would go into great detail with specifics of what my ideal mate would look like, act like, what things she would be into, even down to all of her physical attributes, and many other details. I even named deeper things like the fact that she would need to be very spiritual, business minded, humble, believe in serving others, and not-so-deep things, like the type and length of her hair, body structure, and even the fact that she would be willing to stand up and challenge me on the tough issues. This went on for a week or two, and like most of our game plans, this just sort of settled into a we-will-do-it-whenever-it's-convenient type of thing. Two weeks after we had begun this daily meditation, we had a business convention that we were both planning to attend. About a week prior to leaving, I called a young lady that I had met at a previous convention. We had seen each other several times and had spoken in passing on many occasions, but that was the extent of our knowing each other. We spoke on the phone one day and began communicating nonstop for hours each day until we agreed that we would meet and travel to the convention together. One of the first people that I saw at the convention was my friend. As I approached him, I noticed that he didn't stop to greet me. Instead he just stood there staring with a smile on his face. As I approached him, I noticed that he wasn't looking at me at all; rather, he was staring at the young lady that I was with, and out of pure excitement, he rushed over and picked the young lady up in the air with one arm and screamed, "Senghor, you did it!" At the time, I had no idea what he was referring to that would've caused that type of reaction. He then started to remind me of the conversations we had two weeks earlier after each of our meditation sessions. Keep in mind, this was our first date, and we had only talked on the phone for one week leading up to the convention. So it was very unusual for the first person I introduced her to (a six-foot-two-inch, three-hundred-pound former football player) to walk up, pick her up off her feet with one arm, and scream, "You did it." He then began to repeat back to me the words I had used to describe to him my perfect woman, which fit the description of the woman standing before him, my date. I was astonished when he recounted the very words that had come out of my mouth just two weeks earlier as I looked at and thought about the person standing there with me. Two weeks after this first date, and several weird but very synchronistic events later, we were living together. Two years later, we were married, and a year after that, we had a little girl. The results from that meditation were so astounding that I never did it again, mainly out of fear that the next time my thoughts might be on something that I didn't want versus, in this case, something that I did ultimately want in my life. Had you asked anyone a week prior to this happening, if they saw any of these things in my immediate future, they would have laughed and considered it crazy to even think such a thing. This experience caused me to understand something very powerful about your thoughts. It made me understand that your thoughts, even the subtle ones, once thought about consistently, will come about unless you change them.

The state of your life is nothing more than a reflection of your state of mind.

—Dr. Wayne W. Dyer[80]

Thoughts, like everything else on this planet, in their purest form are simply energy. Energy is alive, and therefore thoughts are alive. Even the most innate objects are just a bunch of tiny subatomic particles of energy, moving and vibrating fast enough to form the solid surface that we see. If you stop to notice how everything responds to your energy, you can easily observe this truth. It is easy to see that everything that is obviously alive responds to everything else that is alive even if it doesn't have motion, like trees, plants, etc. That is why people who show love toward their plants and talk to them have the best results with their gardening. Just like plants, everything else that is alive responds to the mood and attitude of whoever comes in contact with it. Even with the most inanimate objects, like the hunk of metal, screws, rubber, and plastic that we call our automobiles, respond to the energy they're made of and encounter. Certainly you may say to yourself, "There's no way that a car could be considered alive," but how many times have you said to yourself that your car just seems like it drives better right after you've cleaned it? What does cleaning your car have to do with the inner workings of the motor and the way the gears change?

> We need to understand that thoughts are tools. Are we using them as productively as we can? Are our thoughts serving us well, or are we their victims? It's up to us.
>
> —Dr. Tom Morris[81]

I would think absolutely nothing, other than the fact that you show your appreciation for that object, and accordingly it responds to your appreciation by performing better for you. How many times have you heard people say, "My car may not be new, but it gets me from point A to B, and it's more dependable than any new car"? People even name their cars to show their appreciation of them, and those cars keep on chugging along. And the very second that you decide that its time to get rid of that old car that you loved and cared for, it starts acting up. Your thoughts work the exact same way. Your thoughts are alive. I heard a very old recording of a speech that Napoleon Hill gave to a live audience in which he described how he used his thoughts as little messengers, or servants, if you will, to do tasks for him that made his life easier.[82]

He told a doubting reporter this same thing once and explained to him how he was going to send out one of his workers (thoughts) ahead of time to secure him a parking space in the front of a very busy building in the middle of the day. The reporter riding with him assured him that this was the busiest time of day and that it would be nearly impossible to find a parking space in front of this building. As Napoleon pulled toward the building, sure enough, all of the parking spaces were taken. He quickly joked with the passenger that his servant must not have gotten to his request yet, so he would circle around the block. As he turned around the corner, someone was pulling out, and there was his parking space in front of the building, just as he knew it would be prior to leaving his home.[83]

I know what you must be thinking, hearing this story now, but can you imagine what his audience was thinking almost eighty years ago when this speech was given? Or more importantly, can you imagine what the doubting passenger learned that day? Perhaps you're thinking to yourself, *How could someone reach a level of thinking to believe that he could utilize his thoughts in the way just described?* But this is a man who spent the largest part of his life exploring this one aspect of the process of creation. As a matter of fact, I consider him the godfather of self-help.

Napoleon Hill interviewed and studied over five hundred of the wealthiest and most influential people of his time. He was commissioned by the richest man in the world at that time, Andrew Carnegie, after spending a week in his home, to commit a minimum of twenty-five years to study the lives of these people and document what he found. With Carnegie's personal introduction to people like Henry Ford, Thomas Edison, and President Roosevelt, what he learned was profound, so much so that the principles that they all had in common when he reviewed his notes inspired him to write his most famous book about it. This book is probably the first modern exploration of its kind that related to thoughts and how they affect outcomes. His book was entitled *Think and Grow Rich,* and for many of his famous students, that is exactly what they did. What he discovered was that there were six principles that these five hundred people all possessed in common with one another. These six things that they did allowed them to create the legacies that we now read about.[84]

When I heard these six principles described on an original recording of a speech given by Napoleon Hill, I immediately saw that the seven truths were 100 percent in alignment with what he discovered. Here are the six principles that he said would make you rich or would get you anything else you wanted:

1. Fix in your mind the exact amount of money you want.

2. What do you intend to give in exchange for the money you desire?

3. Establish a date you intend to have it.

4. Create a plan for carrying out your desire.

5. Write out a clear statement of your intended desire.

6. Read what you have written out loud at least twice a day—once in the morning and once at night before retiring. As you read, see, feel, and believe that you are already in possession of the money. You must posses a burning desire for its achievement.[85]

Thomas Edison said the application of these steps would not only achieve money but it would be useful for any goal.[86] If you look at the *7 Truths of Life* and compare it to the six principles that Napoleon Hill outlined in his life's work, it's easy to see that the information is almost parallel. There is nothing new under the sun, and the same truths that Napoleon Hill discovered are the same truths being taught here.

Napoleon Hill writes in *Think and Grow Rich:*

> Our brains become magnetized with the dominating thoughts, which we hold in our minds, and, by means with which no man is familiar, these "magnets" attract to us the forces, the people, and the circumstances of life which harmonize with the nature of our dominating thoughts.[87]

When you are committed, the cells in your body are energized by the passion of your purpose.

> Magnetism is one of the prime moving forces in the universe. It is the power that binds the galaxies together. Around every magnet, there is an invisible "magnetic field" of attraction. When a nail comes in contact with this magnetic field, it is drawn to the magnet—as if by magic. The nail has no choice. It never says to itself, "I think I'll ignore the magnetic field today." Did you know that when a nail comes in contact with a permanent magnet, the nail becomes a temporary magnet itself—acquiring powers of attracting that it did not previously possess? As long as the nail remains near the magnet, it retains these new magnetic powers. If the magnet is taken away, the nail returns to its original state. When you examine the atoms of the nail under a microscope, you discover that they possess magnetic attributes, but they are disorganized. The atoms of the nail point in all different directions, and thus cancel out one another's electromagnetic charge. By contrast, the atoms of a magnet are in perfect alignment—their north and south poles face in the same direction. When a magnet attracts a nail, the atoms in the nail begin to line up to match the atoms in the magnet, becoming "like" the magnet. The more aligned these atoms become, the more the ordinary nail behaves like a magnet.
>
> —Mark Victor Hansen and Robert G. Allen[88]

When you apply this statement to what we know about these magnets that Napoleon Hill speaks of, it becomes clear what this statement is meant to convey.

It's this connectivity that I later found that led me to remembering what I had already known but fell out of practice with and thus was experiencing the disconnectedness in the earlier mentioned story referencing the movie *The Legend of Bagger Vance*. As divine of an experience as that was, a few years later, I learned that this experience was only the prelude to a much grander experience.

As I began writing this book, I knew that I wanted to tell the story of how those answers were revealed to me and how I used those four pathways to mastery to get my life back on track, all in the hope that someone else could receive the same benefits as I did. However, I was unaware of the fact that this synchronistic event was just the beginning of a much larger truth being played out in my life. I learned some four years later that the book *The Legend of Bagger Vance* was originally written to expose the Western world to the writing of the holy book of the Hindus, *The Bhagavad Gita*.[89] Junuh, the main character in the movie, played by Matt Damon, was actually representing Arjunuh, the central character in the *Bhagavad Gita*.[90] Bagger Vance, Will Smith's character, actually represented God, and thus his character's name was derived from the name of this holy book, the *Bhagavad-Gita*.[91] I later discovered on a tape series recorded by Dr. Wayne Dyer that the four steps to mastery was the message being bestowed upon Junuh, which is the core message of this holy text.[92] This was all very interesting to me, and I found myself feeling very connected to this entire process as it presented itself in this very detailed but out-of-my-control type of way. As I wrote this book, I continuously had a strong urge to find a copy of the *Bhagavad Gita* and read it. I somehow knew this book was a part of my process of evolution and that I needed to explore beyond the lessons the movie had taught me to find the deeper connection. At the time, I had been traveling back and forth to Jacksonville, Florida, from Atlanta for about two and a half years. I sometimes flew and other times I drove. Often as I drove, I was drawn to this series of billboards advertising this gigantic book depot with over fifty thousand new and used books. One of the buildings of the depot was dedicated to spiritual subject matters. Every time I passed that exit, I would tell myself that I was going to leave early enough to stop and visit that bookstore. Unfortunately, I was in the habit of driving mostly at night, so I always missed my opportunities to stop. I knew whenever I made that stop I would find the copy of the *Bhagavad Gita* that I so desperately wanted to read. Also, I had recently decided to start listening to biblically based tape series about subjects that were similar to the subjects being written about in the book. I guess I figured before I fully committed to telling people the benefits of using the principles of this book, I should check to make certain that it was consistent with the religious text that I was most familiar. I passed this exit for months, never having the opportunity due to timing to stop. As I made this sometimes weekly commute, I became increasingly frustrated that I could never leave in enough time to make it to this exit before the book warehouse closed. Before leaving on my next trip, I made the announcement that we were leaving in enough time to make it to the bookstore to shop. About an hour or two into this trip, I realized that I had misjudged how far we had to drive to get to the exit. This meant I would probably only have a little time to look around for the book and the tapes that I desperately wanted. As I pulled off on the exit and into the parking lot, I noticed that the store was going to close an hour earlier than I expected. This left me with less than an hour to look around. I found several books that I wanted to read but nothing that applied to the subject matters that I wanted to write about. Not to mention, I didn't find the *Bhagavad Gita*. So I left that day disappointed, but I vowed that on my trip returning from Jacksonville back to Atlanta, I would arrive there with hours to shop. This time I knew exactly how far I was away and what time the store would close. I was excited by the anticipation of returning back to the store in two days to find my books. On our returning day, I got up extra early, and I stayed on top of my brothers the entire day. I was determined to finish early and make it to the store. Everything went smoothly that day and just as

I had planned. As we were about to start wrapping things up and get on the road, we received a telephone call from a realtor that we had been waiting to meet with to view several houses. We knew if we didn't take the time to see them, they may not be there our next trip down. We agreed to meet and look at five or six houses very quickly. This would only shave about an hour off my shopping time, so I was still okay. As we saw each house, I continued to remind everyone of the time to ensure we stayed on schedule. As we finished up with the realtor, she received a telephone call concerning three or four more houses that had just hit the market that sounded great. I knew if we looked at those houses, my chance to get to the bookstore in time would be lost. Undaunted, I continued to push everyone along, knowing that even if I only had a few minutes, I would find my books. As we got to the last house, I had pretty much come to the realization that it was going to be very hard to make it to the store and find the books and/or tapes. The last house we came to was in a lot better shape than all of the other houses we viewed that trip. So I figured we could hurry through our evaluation process and make up some time. I was amazed that this house was obviously abandoned yet almost spotless on the inside. More times than not, the houses we walk through require us to wear masks over our faces. We were looking for houses to completely renovate and within the area where we were investing; the houses were over one hundred years old, so we often saw all types of things. But this last house was different; there was no trash on the floor, no signs that people had been sleeping there at night, no needles, and the other usual paraphernalia. This amazed us that there was not one piece of paper or trash in the entire house. As we were walking out of the house, I noticed a custom bookcase with the original glass and knobs still in tact, and for some reason I was drawn to open the cabinet door and look inside. Now, this was something that I was not in the habit of doing, considering you never could tell what would be living inside. But since the inside of the house was so clean, I went ahead and took the chance. I guess it was the loud, "Oh my God" that I yelled that immediately had my two brothers and the realtor turn around and hurry back, for they were almost out the door. There lay in front of me a perfectly preserved copy of the *Bhagavad Gita*. Right beside it lay three very old tape series that were from the early seventies. I opened each tape series, and all the tapes that were inside the cases were in perfect condition. We all stood there in amazement as one of my brothers tried to explain to the realtor our state of shock. As I examined the book to make certain that it was what I had been hoping to find at the bookstore, I was in total awe of what had just transpired. I then took a closer look at the tape series, and the author was a Christian pastor by the name of Joyce Myers. I had never heard of the author, but the fact that I found the three full tape sets by a Christian author, which is something that I was seeking, and the *Bhagavad Gita* at the exact same time was confirmation that these tapes were also an answer to a request. But it wasn't until I read each of the three titles that my speculations were confirmed.

> Work joyfully and peacefully, knowing that right thoughts and right efforts will inevitably bring about right results.
>
> —James Allen[93]

The titles of the tape series were *The Power of Thoughts and Words, The Mind of the Flesh,* and *Managing Your Emotions.* Now, think about what you've been reading. Do you think from just these titles alone I was able to get something that could apply to this work? I was blown away with how in line these tapes were with what was coming through this work. For this reason, I have included a special section highlighting some of the things that I learned from the tape series that were obviously supposed to be a part of the description of the *7 Truths of Life* and their appropriate application.

These events were surreal, in light of the fact I had attempted to get my hands on this book for months. As I drove pass the exit that night, I remember thinking how awesome God is and how perfect the universe had been designed. It is always ready and able to provide us with all of the tools we need to pursue our life's purpose.

Proverbs 23:7–As a man thinketh in his heart so does he become. In other words we are today the product of yesterday's thoughts.

Mathew 6:25–34–take no thought for tomorrow saying what shall we eat and what shall we wear and what shall we and so on and so on. If the thought comes don't take it because the Bible says you will have what you say.

Psalms 19–14 Let the words of my mouth and the meditation of my heart be acceptable in your sight oh God. Heart and Mind are almost inseparable. What you meditate in your heart is what you think on.

Mark 24–Be careful what you are hearing–for the measure of thought and study that you give to the truth that you hear is the measure of virtue and knowledge and will come back to you again. Be careful how long you think on what you hear.

Faith is seeing it done ahead of time–If all you see is doubt that it will come about how can you expect that it will come about?

Don't prejudge something–just because something didn't work the 1st time doesn't mean it's not going to happen for you this time. Just your knowledge of this changes who you are and if you are not who you were before then don't think that you are going to get the same results. Don't judge what you are going to do–Judge what you are doing–Know thy self.

The Bible says–if we will judge ourselves that we won't come under divine judgment. Never give your opinion in less someone asks you for it.

—Joyce Myers[94]

To summarize this chapter, there are just a few things that require mastering before the application of the following truth can take place. First, make certain that you have answered the question, "What are your dreams?" Then ask yourself, "Have I clearly identified them?" Once you have the answers to both of these questions the next step is to live out of your imagination, not your memory, because the past does not have to equal your future. In this way, you must remember to use selective thinking. Selective thinking is the ability to remember to forget. So the quickest way to settle down and stop bringing yourself such a wide variety of experiences is simply to stop changing your mind or allowing others to change your mind so often about whom you are and what you desire.

Dr. Wayne Dyer once made this observation after three decades of teaching these principles: "I have found that people who have a passion or a strong will for what they want to achieve, and who do not allow others to smear their inner pictures of what they want to manifest, always seem to get what they desire in their lives."[95]

As mentioned earlier in this chapter, the mind works in pictures, not words. Words are powerful, but remember, a picture is worth a thousand words. Therefore, what you say to yourself is important, but what you visualize in your mind is even more important, and it is for this reason that the next truth, truth number five, follows this truth. Undoubtedly, you are what you think about all day long, and what you think about all day long will eventually be displayed in the words that you speak. You see, all states of mind produce themselves first in the words that you utter. This is the reason why you must preselect words that support what you want, which is the next truth, truth number five.

Truth #5

You must speak words that are
in support of what you want

- Application: You must intentionally choose words that support what you have decided you want, which support the beliefs you have, which support the goals you have set, and then support the thoughts you have prechosen to think.

- Explanation: The thoughts you think will eventually become the words you speak, so you must choose your words carefully, for your mouth is the physical expression of your internal dialogue.

- Manifesting Principle: You must create I Am affirmations and incantations that speak words that are a reflection of who you are and what you are now choosing to be. An affirmation affirms that which you choose to be true in your life.

  These truths used together will design your life plan for manifesting:

  Truth #1: The first step to getting what you want is you must identify what it is that you want.

  Truth #2: You must develop beliefs that are in support of your receiving what you want.

  Truth #3: You must set goals that are in support of what you want.

Truth #4: You must think thoughts that are in support of what you want.

Truth #5: You must speak words that are in support of what you want.

We have now reached a really critical point in the process of creation and the application of the highest aspects of each truth for the manifestation of your desires. This process of creation begins with truth number four: thinking thoughts that are in support of what you want. But as you can see, the three previous truths must also be a part of this process in order for manifestation to take place. This next truth follows this same process because the things you speak about originate from the thoughts you have. The words you speak have a profound impact on the things that come to pass in your life. The reason why the words you speak are so impactful is they represent the thoughts you think, the plans you've made, the beliefs you have, and the desires you seek. That is why this truth comes after truth number four. It is vitally important to understand the power of the spoken word. Each word you speak is a confession or a confirmation of all the previous truths and is a direct representation of the thoughts you think.

Every word that is spoken exercises a power in personal life, and that power will work either for or against the person, depending upon the nature of the word.

—*Christian Larson*[96]

Choose your words carefully, for what you say is a confirmation of what you are verbalizing as reality in your life. This is your way of saying, "Yes. This is what I want, this is what I believe, this is how I will go about it, and this is what I think is so." Words are so powerful because they're an expression of many different aspects of whom and what you are. It is for this reason that you can always tell the beliefs, attitudes, thoughts, and desires of a person and much more by the words he or she chooses to speak. Your words are an expression of all the other truths that preceded this one.

There are two things that give your words creative power. The first is the fact that what you speak confirms and furthers the creative process of the things that you think, which originates from the other previous truths. The second being, you are the first person who hears the words that come out of your mouth. This is the reason that I tell people that the quickest way to truly learn something is to teach it. Once taught is twice learned, for you're the first person to hear the words that you speak. The things you talk about will always come about. They are a reflection of your wants, your beliefs, your plans, and your thoughts. If not guarded, we will often find our words just as loosely chosen and thrown around as the thoughts we have. This does not present a problem for those that are already living their purpose and have found their passions in life. Most likely, they're thinking and speaking words that further propel them in the direction they're already headed. However, for the other 95 percent of the population, this presents a challenge that must be overcome if they are to gain control over their life and intentionally design the life they seek to live.

A man shall eat good by the fruit of his mouth.

Proverbs 13:2[97]

The problem is most people often talk about what they think about even if it's not a representation of what they want. Have you ever thought something long enough and you knew it was not something that you wanted to say but said it by accident anyway? This creates a real dilemma since thoughts are random and they come and go, and most are not even ours. However, each word you speak is yours and yours alone. The thoughts that scroll through your mind all have the possibility of making their way out of your mouth in the form of a spoken word. Obviously, this places a huge responsibility on that hole in the center of your face called a mouth. It's your words that tell the universe which thoughts you are choosing to affirm as yours. Of the thousands of thoughts that run through your mind each day, it's the several hundred words that you choose to speak that tell the universe, and everyone else, which thoughts are truly yours and which are not. That is what gives your words their power and you must gain control of this power by constantly monitoring the words you speak.

As thoughts go into the queue for furthering the process of creation, they are transferred into expressed words. It is this truth that gives them life. This is why throughout time, in nearly every spiritual text ever written, there have been warnings relating to the words that we speak. In the Bible, in the book of Proverbs, verses 18–21, it says that "death and life are in the power of the tongue and they that love it shall eat the fruit there of."[98] What this verse is teaching us is that we have the ability to speak life or death into any endeavor that we seek to take on, and those that are careful with it will reap the benefits of it. This reminds me of one of the many times that I created what I wanted to have in my life just to turn around and see the whole thing fall apart in the same remarkable fashion as I received it.

If you remember, in the beginning of the book, I performed a test to make certain that what these seven truths teach is real and that just by applying the message of this book, one can manifest the desires of one's heart. I did that test and achieved my goal by acquiring several homes, in particular, the last home, right before my thirty-fourth birthday. A short time later, I bought that house and began the process of renovating. About three or four months into the project, my business partner decided that he wanted out of the deal, so I decided to purchase the house out of our jointly owned trust for myself, which was not part of my original plan. As I mentioned before, my previous house sold very quickly, so as far as I could tell, things were still going well. Not more than a month later, a developer, who originally owned the land that this house and seven other homes sat on, drained the fifteen-acre lake that we shared. Since I had decided to purchase the house and live there, I began all types of upgrades that were not part of the original plan, which was to renovate the house and sell it. One of the upgrades required the removal of half an acre of trees from the back of the house to enhance the view of the lake from any part of the house. Not only did the developer drain the lake, but he moved several million gallons of water down the road to another subdivision and began calling that new subdivision lakefront property. Ironically, just a week earlier, that subdivision had no water. As you can imagine, this created a major eyesore. We went from having a beautiful lake with water stretching almost as far as the eye can see to a mosquito-infested swamp that could now be seen from nearly every room in the house. This scene made me sick to my stomach every time I looked at it. To add insult to injury, we had to launch a major class action lawsuit against the developer, costing a ton of money and time.

As I looked out and saw what was becoming of what could've potentially been my dream home, without realizing it, I began to focus all of my attention on what I didn't want, and boy, did I get a bunch of that. Everything that was right about this deal turned wrong. I began to argue with the attorneys, my business partner, my wife, and anyone else associated with this house. I now was openly complaining that this was the worst deal I had ever been involved in. Prior to this deal, I never had to go to court and be involved in any lawsuit as it related to my real estate business. But because of this deal, I was in court almost once a month. Five different lawsuits came about in less than six months. I was suing people, and I was being sued. I eventually gave up and decided I would sell the house and cut my losses. Due to the lake situation, the house had now lost over two hundred thousand dollars in value, which made it almost impossible to sell. As I look back on the collapse of what seemed to be the most perfect deal I had ever been involved in that fell into my lap, it turned out to be the worst deal with just as many synchronistic things going wrong as originally went right. It took me a long time to realize that both scenarios were my doing. I remember changing from wanting to live in this house to wanting to move out. I changed my beliefs, plans, thoughts, and the words I chose to speak. They all reflected the opposite of what I wanted. Even knowing this, I was somehow still surprised when just as magically as this deal came together, it unraveled.

Every Problem Has a Solution

With every problem, its opposite, the solution, must exist. To effectively address the trouble that our mouths can get us into, God created a safety net in this creative process—the freedom to choose what you allow to come out of it. Just because you think something doesn't mean you have to say it. Naturally, if your mouth is just as unpredictable as your mind, then this has the potential of presenting a major obstacle. The solution to this problem is to guard your tongue and make certain that the words that come out of your mouth confirm and further the creation of that which you desire. Initially, this will require a constant monitoring of what you speak. As you begin to catch yourself saying things that don't accurately reflect who you are or who you're choosing to be, simply choose to say the opposite. Now, this constant thinking before you speak may sound like a grueling task, but once you have done it for a few days, it actually becomes quite fun.

The second way to master this is to prechoose the words that are reflective of who you are and who you are choosing to be. Most things we say repeatedly, we say out of habit. Therefore, we must begin habitually saying things that bring more of what we choose versus its opposite. When people ask you how you're doing, what is your habitual response? Is it "I'm getting by" or "I'm doing all right" or "I guess it's not as bad as it could be"? Do any of these statements sound familiar? Even if such responses are true statements of how you currently feel, are they a reflection of how you would like for it to be in the near future? If it is, then continue saying it and you will continue getting the same as you speak. If it is not, then you need to pick new automatic responses to habitual questions. Thus, when someone asks how you're doing, give him or her the response that's a reflection of where you want to be. Tell him or her you are outstanding and getting better by the minute or anything else that's a reflection of where you would like to be. You see, this is not about being dishonest with yourself or trying to trick yourself—because we both know this is impossible—but it is about looking for the silver lining in what you're going through and focusing on getting more of what's good in your life and expanding that. Invariably, you always have a choice to reflect on the good or the bad; whichever one you choose will expand. Even at your lowest point, there is still always something to be thankful for. This reminds me of a story I read about a high-powered executive who lost his job and a large sum of money and thus decided to commit suicide. When they did his autopsy, they were amazed to see how all of his major organs were in the condition of a thirty-year-old even though he was well into his sixties. When I think about this story, I wonder if this guy had any idea that he had been blessed in this way. If he had known, would he have continued to focus on the bad or would he have found the silver lining and focused on the good?

Another habitual response is the need to match the other person's disposition. When someone who's negative approaches someone who's not, the tendency is for the positive person to down play his position, if not to abandon his position all together. This is done so the other person is not made to feel worse than he's already feeling. Unfortunately, this only takes the other person further down in the nonproductive direction. Rather than thinking you're helping this person by doing this, understand that the more you take yourself down to his level, the more you hurt both you and him. No one benefits in this exchange, so you must find a new automatic response when this scenario presents itself.

There are many more examples of automatic responses than have been conveyed here, but it's your job to identify the ones that are a part of your daily speech and measure them to see if they empower or disempower you. Once you identify your habitual spoken responses to comments made and to situations that continuously show up, measure them and change the ones that are disempowering. Carefully look at each of these situations and begin to write out the most powerful responses you can muster up to each of the settings you repeatedly find yourself in. Everyone has his or her own set of circumstances that make this exercise appropriate for him or her. Some people work jobs that often cause them to defend their reasons for choosing their line of work. Or maybe you have chosen a hobby or a spouse or anything that causes people to ask you the same or similar types of questions that trigger an inclination in you to downplay your position.

> Always tell the truth–it's the quickest way to freedom and enlightenment.
>
> —Anonymous

I often found myself doing this in my line of work because it was my job to teach people how to be better at what I did than I was. This was often met with a lot of reasoning that would appear on the surface as compliments yet underneath were really excuses for people not to exceed their own expectations. In an effort to keep the people I worked with motivated, I often had to find ways to let them know that we were no different, and what I could do, they too could do. The key was to do this without belittling myself in the process. I learned to replace my habitual responses by acknowledging what the person said and letting him or her know that I received the compliment while not letting that be an excuse for him or her to think that he or she couldn't achieve the same as I. For example, I would often hear people make the comment jokingly, "If I had your hand, I would cut mine off." This is a pretty popular saying designed to tell someone that he's got it good, and my automatic response was always, "If you cut your hands off for mine, you would just be handless." Now, what was I really saying to this person? What I was really saying was that he was wrong. Not only did they not want my hands, but they would be better off having no hands if they chose to have mine. Or another example is when someone would say, "You the man," then I would say, "No, you the man" or "I'm not the man, but I wish I were." Do you see how this is nonbeneficial to both parties? I never forget telling one of my friends, "Hey, you the man," and he said, "Thanks. I'm so glad you noticed." I thought to myself, *Who in the hell does this guy think he his?* Then I realized he was telling me, "Yes, you're right. I am the man" and that this was what he was choosing to have in his life. Once you have identified which automatic responses are not in support of you, begin to replace the disempowering ones with your new, empowering habitual responses.

A wholesome tongue is a tree of life.

Proverbs 15:4

Preselecting Your Words Through Affirmations

Preselecting your words to support your desires before speaking them will enable you to manifest that which is not currently so. The manifesting principle of this truth is that you must create affirmations that are in support of the things that you want while using the two most powerful words ever spoken in this process of creation. The words *I am* and any words that follow will be so. As you can see, the words that come out of your mouth confirm the other truths, as previously described. The words *I am* preceding your prechosen words serve as commands that tell the universe that this is what is true for you. And the universe confirms what you are saying as true for you by making it come to pass.

I remember riding on a plane while reading a book entitled *Three Magic Words* by U.S. Anderson. As I came to the very last page, where the author had waited the entire book to disclose what the three magic words were, I was overwhelmingly surprised and excited as I read them and closed the book. Now, because I am hoping that you will take the time to find this book and read it, I'm not going to share here what those three magic words were, but I wasn't able to do the same with the lady sitting in the seat next to me. She told me that she couldn't help herself after reading the title and watching the expression on my face as I completed the book; she

just had to know what those three magic words were. As I flipped
back to the last page that only had those three words printed there
in big, bold letters, she stared and kept insisting that I tell her what
the three magic words were. I explained to her that if I told her what
the three words were, it would spoil it for her and that perhaps she
should pick the book up and read it. She explained to me that after
watching the expression of exaltation totally take over my face and
my entire body that she couldn't wait. She told me that she loved
books that were empowering, and she promised that she would buy
and read the book; nevertheless, she had to know what had gotten
me so excited. We had talked earlier in the flight for some time, and
she was a very sweet lady, yet I really didn't want to spoil the end for
her. Since she demanded, I reluctantly handed her the book. She
quickly opened the book up to the last page, and I watched to see if
she would light up the way that I had. As she read the three words
printed on the page, she just sat there holding the book and staring
at the three words; she then closed the book, handed it back to me,
and never said another word to me the entire flight. I wanted to ask
her if what she read offended her and if she wanted to discuss it,
but she seemed very disturbed. She even looked around, as if to see
if maybe there were some additional seats open on the plane so she
could move. I never said anything and neither did she. The only clue
I will give you is that the first two of these three magic words are *I
am*. The point of the book was to express how these words summon
the most creative force in the universe to our beckoning call and that
you can fill in the third word. You will have to get the book to find
out what the author said on the last page that was true for him and
what he was hoping would have been discovered by the reader.

As we venture forward, I think it's incredibly important to define
what an affirmation is and how it's used as part of this process of
manifestation. Affirmations are used to affirm things, so you should
use them accordingly. When you affirm something, you are telling
the universe that the words you speak are what is. This is how I define
proper prayer: being thankful that your prayers are being answered
even before they are asked. Proper prayer will be discussed in a later

chapter as part of the description of the seventh truth, where a better explanation of why this principle works will be provided. You must create "I am" affirmations that support what you have identified as the object of your desire. This commandment tells the universe what is true for you and that you are now instructing the universe to make it so. That's how strong those two words and whatever you put behind them are. Why else do you think that God is called the great I AM in almost every religion on this planet? Because God is the Creator and I AM is another name for that which creates. Therefore, using these commanding words before prechosen words that support what you choose to be is the manifesting principle of this truth. Also, bear in mind that "I am," coupled with that which you don't desire, will assist in manifesting that as well. When you say things like I am sick, tired, fat, sorry, broke, or anything else that is not a reflection of who and what you want to be, you call it forth. So don't blame God, the devil, your parents, or anyone else for the things that you have made a reality in your life. Find and develop affirmations that are true for you and describe what you desire and then repeat them out loud and in your mind as often as you can. Napoleon Hill said in his book *Think and Grow Rich*, "Repetition of affirmations of orders to your subconscious mind is the only known method of voluntary development of the emotion of faith."[100] Create your own affirmations or find ones that resonate with you and repeat them daily.

The lips of the righteous feed many.

Proverbs 10:21[101]

The following meditation is an affirmation from U.S. Andersen's book *Three Magic Words* that stuck with me, and I repeated it daily for years. I believe it affirms purposely speaking words that support what you want.

I Am Meditation

I know that I am pure spirit, that I always have been and that I always will be. There is inside of me a place of confidence, and quietness, and security, where all things are known and understood. This is the Universal mind, God, of which I am a part of and which responds to me, as I ask of it. This Universal mind knows the answer to all of my problems, and even now the answers are speeding their way to me. I needn't struggle for them; I needn't worry or strive for them. When the time comes, the answers will be there. I give my problems to the great mind of God; I let go of them, confident that the correct answers will return to me when they are needed. Through the great law of attraction, everything in life that I need for my work and fulfillment will come to me. It is not necessary that I strain about this, only believe. For in the strength of my belief, my faith will make it so. I see the hand of divine intelligence all about me, in the flower, the tree, the brook, the meadow. I know that the intelligence that created all these things is in me and around me, and that I can call upon it for my slightest need. I know that my body is a manifestation of pure spirit and that spirit is perfect; therefore, my body is perfect also. I enjoy life, for each day brings a constant demonstration of the power and wonder of the Universe and myself. I am confident. I am serene. I am sure. No matter what obstacle or undesirable circumstance crosses my path, I refuse to accept it, for it is nothing but illusion. There can be no obstacle or undesirable circumstance to the mind of God, which is in me, and around me, and serves me now.[102]

This meditation sums up all the truths that have come before this and applies to all the truths that follow it. Each of the "I am" affirmations of this meditation speaks to the highest parts of you and allows you to activate all of the creative power of the universe.

One of the greatest examples of a person who consistently used an "I Am" affirmation is Muhammad Ali. Every time he spoke his now-famous words, "I am the greatest," he was making a statement to the universe of what was so, and he became what he spoke. Not to rehash Ali's entire story but below are highlights of his accomplishments that validate the power of this affirmation:

As an amateur boxer, Ali attracted notice in 1960 by winning the Amateur Athletic Union light heavyweight and Golden Gloves Heavyweight Championships. At the Rome Olympics, also in 1960, Ali crushed his opponents to win a gold medal in the light heavyweight division. After turning pro, Ali defeated his first opponents. Then on February 25, 1964, he fought and knocked out Sonny Liston in seven rounds, thus becoming the new heavyweight world champion. Ali defended his title nine times from 1965 to 1967 and became universally recognized as the world heavyweight champion after out pointing World Boxing Association (WBA) champion Ernie Terrell in fifteen rounds on February 6, 1967. Ali often proclaimed his invincibility when he boasted, "I am the greatest!" After defending his heavyweight title six times, including a third fight with Joe Frazier, Ali lost it to Leon Spinks on February 15, 1978, in a split decision. He regained the WBA title from Spinks seven months later in a unanimous decision, becoming the first boxer to win the heavyweight championship three times. In 1979, Ali announced his retirement, at that point having lost only three times in fifty-nine fights, but he returned to fight World Boxing Council champion Larry Holmes in 1980 and Trevor Berbick of Canada in 1981, losing both. Ali then retired permanently.[103]

Most boxing experts argue about what made Ali so great. Some think it was his unusual boxing style. Others argue it was his speed and crafty footwork. However, all unanimously agree that it was his trash talking that encouraged him, his fans, and discouraged his opponents. "I am the greatest" was all that he spoke and was what he believed, and therefore he was.

As you complete truth number five, it should be easy to see what comes next in this evolutionary process of creation since each truth is logically leading to the natural progression of the other one. In this process, our thoughts eventually become our words, and our words become our deeds, which are our actions. And this is truth number six: you must choose actions that are in support of your getting what you are after.

Truth #6

You must take actions that are in support of what you want.

- Application: You must intentionally choose actions that support what you have decided that you want. These actions should support your beliefs, goals, thoughts, and the words you speak.

- Explanation: Your actions are the byproduct of all the preceding truths, but it is this truth where your words are made flesh and dwell amongst us. This is the deed in the thought, word, and deed trilogy and is the physical manifestation of all the truths that came before it.

- Manifesting Principle: To help someone else experience within himself that which you wish to experience within yourself is the highest action that you can take.

    These truths used together will design your life plan for manifesting:

    Truth #1: The first step to getting what you want is to identify what it is that you want.

    Truth #2: You must develop beliefs that are in support of your getting what you want.

    Truth #3: You must set goals that are in support of what you want.

Truth #4: You must think thoughts that are in support of what you want.

Truth #5: You must speak words that are in support of what you want.

Truth #6: You must take actions that are in support of what you want.

Your actions are just a reflection of a combination of all of the truths that came before this one. By this time you should be on auto pilot towards accomplishing the things you desire for yourself. However the question is are you heading in the direction of your choice or are you traveling the course set by someone or something else. If you have applied the truths discussed thus far and developed the life plan created by the application of each truth, than you are more than on your way to the destination that you outlined in the very first chapter of this book. As you can now see each truth led you to the discovery of the next truth. This process will develop a seamless series of supporting principles that will catapult you towards the destiny of your choosing.

> *Do not wait; the time will never be "just right." Start where you stand, and work with whatever tools you may have at your command, and better tools will be found as you go along.*
>
> —*Napoleon Hill*[104]

Do You

Few people struggle with the application of this truth. It rarely presents a problem for people when they realize all of the benefits that come from helping other people. But it is not often understood that if you can help enough people get the things they want in life, then automatically you will end up with the things you want in life. Whether you have been exposed to the deeper workings of this truth, or not just embracing this will always guide you toward the best actions to take on your personal journey toward your own defined success. I often tell people that the best way to help someone else is to help yourself first. Someone once said that "a drowning man can't save a drowning man."

> In this interconnected universe, every improvement we make in our private world improves the world at large for everyone.
>
> —Dr. Wayne Dyer[105]

Be self-centered; serve yourself first. Do what's absolutely best for you at all times. Sounds like bad advice, doesn't it? Whenever you choose to take the highest action for yourself, it always serves everyone else. As counterintuitive as it may seem, that which serves you also serves the world as a whole. However, let's just examine this further. Imagine a person who is serving herself at all costs. If this person was satisfying all of her heart's desires, do you see how this person would most likely be very fulfilled and happy? This person would obviously be a pleasure to be around, for she would have little to complain or be mad about. This person would love herself to no end and would most likely be in a position to serve others. If you can imagine that, then could you go as far as to imagine a group of people or even an entire country where, at minimum, all of their basic desires are met? Can you see the implications? Can you imagine a whole country of people like our before-described Mrs. Happy Go Lucky? On the flip side, let's imagine the person who has the exact opposite going on in his life. Even if this person chose to serve others, not having acquired any of the desires of his heart, he will still end up being a person who doesn't have a lot to offer, not just physically but also emotionally.

One might assume this to be so, for surely you can't give something away that you yourself don't possess. However, the quickest way to possess something you don't have is to learn to give it away. By offering someone something that you don't possess, you tell the universe that you have it to give. This is being thankful in advance for that which has not happened yet, which is the seventh and final truth that we will discuss in the next chapter. Exactly how do you give something that you don't have? You reverse the normal process of creation and begin acting as if what you seek already is. You go ahead and experience the feelings of having that which you seek. Miraculously, you will soon find yourself in possession of it. Perhaps this sounds like some type of play on words, but these two opposite truths can exist in the same place as one, which is the definition of a divine dichotomy. By reversing the process, manifestation takes place. Most people think that if they perform a certain action that they will have a certain thing, and then they will be whatever end result they are after. This process is backward. This process says that if you do, you will have, and then this will cause you to be, when it's actually the reverse of this. To truly take the right actions and assist in this process of manifestation, you have to be first and then do, and then you will have. Now, let me explain the way this process works. Most people believe that if you *do* a lot of work, then you will *have* a lot of things, and thus you will *be* happy. Nonetheless, by reversing this process, you actually manifest the things that you desire into your life versus creating them. You first must decide to *be* happy, and you will joyfully *do* the things necessary to support your state, and thus you will *have* that which you seek. By doing this, your actions will always be in support of what you want and never in support of what you don't want.

> Kindness in words creates confidence,
> Kindness in thinking creates profoundness,
> Kindness in giving creates love.
>
> —Lao Tzu[106]

The Manifesting Principle

The highest action that you can take is to help someone else experience in him or herself that which you wish to experience in yourself.

What does this mean and how does this apply to you? We are all familiar with the old clichés that center around this subject. Clichés like, "You get what you give," "You reap what you sow," and "What goes around comes around." What most people have written off as just another catchy saying or a cliché, I find to be some of our highest truths. To apply this manifesting principle, you must find someone that you can assist in the attainment of his goals and in turn you will accomplish your goals. This is the manifesting principle. The reason this works is because what you do for someone else, you also do for yourself. In this way, you get back far more than you give. Every time you assist someone in experiencing what he desires, you send the universe a clear message that you have that to give. Do this with someone who seeks something similar to what you seek repeatedly and you will manifest it in your life. This is why a mentoring relationship is just as beneficial to the mentee as it is to the mentor. The person who seeks your mentoring obviously knows that what you do is in alignment with what he desires and so by helping him get what he desires, you also further yourself in that same arena.

Understand this truth requires balance, and it also requires you to take part in the largest aspect of giving, which is receiving. If you are always giving but don't allow people to give to you, then you just missed your biggest opportunity to give. Your biggest opportunity to give is to allow others to give to you. That's giving within itself. Subsequently, when you hoard what you have or close yourself down to the opportunity to receive, you take away someone else's opportunity to give. It is said that a closed hand can't give or receive. This was especially difficult for me to learn, mainly because I enjoyed giving, but I always found it very hard to allow someone to give to me. I was always reluctant to receive not only physical things but compliments as well.

Another way to align with the manifesting principle is by deciding upfront what you plan to give in exchange for what you wish to receive. What do you plan to sow for the harvest that you seek to reap? Just as it is in nature, there is a time for sowing and a time for reaping. It is for this reason as part of the process of developing your life plan that we suggest that you complete the circle by deciding what you will support in advance for receiving your desires as you apply the truths contained in these pages. Then actually give a minimum of 10 percent of whatever you create through this process back to a charity of your choice and teach others how to do the same. This enables you to complete the process and become its owner, for once taught is truly twice learned. Remember, the very act of giving something away reinforces the realization that you have it to give away. You cannot give to another something you don't have.

> There is one who scatters–yet increases all the more, and there is one who withholds more than his justly due, but it results only in Poverty.
>
> Proverbs 11:24[107]

Applying the Manifesting Principle

Act as if you are and you will draw it to you. What you act as if you are, you become. People who pretend to be a certain thing end up becoming it because by pretending you are that which you wish to become, you tell the universe in undeniably strong terms that this is who you choose to be. This is why when kids pretend to be something in play long enough, they begin to develop the things that they need to become what they are imitating. If this process of make-believe is supported by the parents, they will experience being that faster than if it is unsupported. Parents that watch to see what their kids take an interest in and support it should look closer into the things that they do when they play pretend. The things that you see them do on the surface that are in their physical space, like playing with toys, watching a particular show, or singing to their favorite songs doesn't require them to use what we have already determined is the most creative force in the universe: desire. But when they pretend, it is the desire to do or have something that is not there that makes this usage of a child's imagination even possible. Be attentive to your children's make-believe games, and you will develop a clearer sense of the activities, if supported, that may bring them closer to living their purpose. When you examine all of the greatest athletes, entertainers, artists, and any other profession that draws lots of attention, all of the people that are at the top of these professions pretended to be what they currently are. I have read story after story where each person recounted how he or she always stood in the mirror and pretended to be his or her favorite star or he or she played by him or herself, pretending to be a person who excelled in what he or she currently does. It may serve your discovery process well if you try to remember what you pretended to be.

It is said in the book *Conversations with God,* "Act as though you are separate from nothing, and no one, and you will heal your world tomorrow."[108] This is the greatest secret of all time. You get what you give; what goes around comes around; you reap what you sow. Understanding the above statements and the preceding truth allows you to fully understand and capitalize on the manifesting principle for truth number six.

Understand that it is about power with, not power over.

—Neale Donald Walsch[109]

When you truly understand that what you do for someone else you automatically do yourself, applying this truth becomes a cinch, for we are all connected, and even if you don't believe that this is true, it will do you good to act as if you do.

Fear Is Conquered By Action

I'm sure you will agree that the number one reason people don't take action is not because they don't know what to do; it's because they don't do what they know. Then what is it that keeps people from doing what they know and taking the right actions instead of procrastinating, especially when faced with the decision to move their lives forward? This is extremely critical because no matter how much something impacts you or how much it has benefited you to learn, it has absolutely no value if you don't take action and utilize it. People often say that knowledge is power, but I have learned that knowledge in and of itself is potential power. It is applied knowledge that holds the true power. Typically, there are only two reasons people don't apply the things that they learn and know will benefit them. It's either fear or lack of understanding of how to proceed that keeps people paralyzed when faced with the task of applying new information. Fortunately, fear, we have learned, can quickly be fixed. Lack of belief requires a little more diligence. People have two main fears in this area: the fear of change and the fear of failure. Both of these fears are easily conquered by taking action. As a matter of fact, action is the only remedy to fear.

Tony Robbins is the master of teaching how to conquer fear through taking action. He built his entire career and became famous by tapping into people's ability to overcome any fear by taking action. He developed countless ways to convince people to simply and very easily take action when faced with something that they feared. Amazingly, before millions of people's eyes, a person's fears (sometimes very painful and paralyzing fears) would just melt away. He was so convinced that action would conquer fear 100 percent of the time that he challenged any doctor that had clients that suffered from chronic illnesses due to some type of fear such as heights, spiders, rejection, or anything else, that he could cure them. Not only did he claim that he could cure them, he challenged doctors to bring clients that had been receiving treatment for years, and he would cure them within a ridiculous time, like ten minutes. He then told each of the psychologists that he would do this on television for the entire world to see. As you can imagine, this was something that people wanted to see, and the patients who agreed to be treated by Tony Robbins, who had no medical training, or any other kind of training for that matter, were just as anxious to be cured. I know that there is genius in boldness, but I thought that this was insanity. Just imagine if he failed at this after telling people on the radio, in the newspapers, and on national television to bring any ailment that was fear based and he would heal them permanently in ten minutes.

That could've been a career ender for him. Quite frankly, it could've possibly landed him in jail if anyone got hurt while he attempted to cure them even though they had volunteered to go through with it. Happily, we know his career didn't end, and he is one of the biggest motivational speakers ever, thanks to the success of this experiment that catapulted him there. As each person came on stage, he had already reviewed their debilitating fear and was prepared to treat him or her. Time after time, he would simply convince people to take an action that would lead not only to facing their fear but eventually to conquering it. For instance, if they had a fear of snakes, he would help them conquer that fear by having them to touch and even hold the snake. Maybe they had a fear of heights; he would immediately take them to the top floor of the building and have them face that fear with action. As silly as this may sound, and even though this made common sense, it was still hard to believe it worked. Astoundingly, it not only worked on some of the patients, it worked on all of them. Thus, he proved time and time again that confronting your fears with action is all it takes to overcome them.[110]

Now you may be asking yourself, "If it's that easy, then why pay thousands of dollars to be treated for fears that could be overcome by just going to a Tony Robbins seminar?" Your guess is as good as mine. Why do most people hold themselves back when they've been given the answers to the questions that are required for the fulfillment of their desires? When you find the answer to this question, you will have the ingredients to change the world!

> Success is often gained by not doing. The Strategy is as much in knowing what not to do and when not to do it as it is in knowing what to do and when to do it.
>
> —Sun Tzu[111]

Taking the Right Actions

Fear of change and fear of failure are the two most debilitating fears when it comes to your personal success. Now that we have discovered that action is the cure for this, it's now time to explore just what types of actions we need to take that are in alignment with your desires and will help you overcome the fears that have held you where you are.

The first thing you must understand about taking the right action is that sometimes no action is the right action. Understanding the ebb and flow of your own personal success is one of the most important aspects of taking the right actions. Taking the right actions requires you to take action during the right times, which makes them the right actions at the right times. Precisely what does this mean and how does it work? The days that you wake up feeling like you are ready to take on the world and that you can do no wrong are the days when you are in your flow, and the days when you feel like you have two left feet are the days that you are in your ebb. Everything in life has its cycles, and they operate in this same ebb and flow. Whether it's nature, the lunar cycles, or your personal moods, they all have a rhythm that they operate from. This dialogue is designed to help you remember what you want to do and how to do it. Timing is everything, and by understanding your personal ebbs and flows, you will create the right actions at the right time.

> Don't let what you cannot do interfere with what you can do.
>
> —John Wooden[112]

Your body tells you by the way you feel whether you are in an ebb or a flow. You have to stop and take notice of these different times in order to discover your patterns. Learn to observe when what you are doing comes easily and when you struggle to do things that would normally happen with very little effort. Do you work best at night or during the day, in the morning or in the afternoon? Is there a point in the day that you seem more drained than energized? Is there a time, like at daybreak or sunset, that you feel inspired? The time of the day, week, or the month that you feel most inspired and energized is the time that you should focus on the creative part of what you're working on. Once you become aware of your high-energy times, you should begin to schedule your big meetings, presentations, and any other major aspect of your game plan during this period as much as possible. It makes sense to plan your most important activities during the times you are at your best or in your flow. The days that you wake up saying, "The world better beware because I'm going to bring it" are the days you should make your most important calls and try to do your most critical activities. The days when you get out of bed and wish you could get back in and stay there are not the days to take on the critical activities, if you can avoid them. I especially noticed this during the process of writing this book. When I woke early in the morning or found myself up late at night writing, the ideas flowed and words seemed to find themselves on the paper with little to no effort on my part. I figured out that this was my time, and I could get three or four times as much done as I could during the times that I attempted to work on writing the book in the middle of the day while trying to stay on schedule. The harder I tried, the less I seemed to get done. I found myself working for five or six hours and accomplishing very little. I could've worked for one or two hours during the right time and achieved more instead of wasting countless hours and energy.

> There is a time for being ahead.
> There is a time for being behind.
> There is a time for being in motion.
> There is a time for being at rest.
> There is a time for being vigorous.
> There is a time for being exhausted.
>
> —Dr. Wayne Dyer[113]

After one month of monitoring your ebb and flow times, you will see a pattern begin to emerge that will give you the outline for when and how to plan your work, play, and the pursuit of your desires. Continue to monitor and you will begin to see an even larger scope of what months are for your sowing and which are for your reaping. Scheduling your work around these times as much as you possibly can and in as many ways as you can will manifest your success with little effort or struggle on your part. This is a part of the ebb and flow process that everything on this planet undergoes. There is a season for everything on this planet, and understanding your season is vital to your success or the lack thereof.

In Proverbs it suggests, "Do not ignore the ant." In other words, don't be ig-nor-ant. Proverbs 6:6–8 says, "Go to the ant, o sluggard, observe her ways and be wise, which, having no chief, officer or ruler, prepares her food in the summer, and gathers her provision in the harvest."[114] This proverb tells us to study the life of the ant and we will understand how this tiny insect lives in balance with all that is, and as you observe her ways, you can too. The ant knows which times are for sowing and which times are for reaping. I once watched a special on television about ants and how the United States government, as well as other military forces, studied how the ants organized themselves in battle.[115] I watched the ants work together to accomplish strategic goals, sacrificing one for the good of all, and I thought to myself, *Boy, if we humans could only be as smart as these ants, we could reverse the damage that we have done to our world.* As I continued to watch the program, I realized that the reason why the military was studying these ants was for a totally different purpose than the one I had derived. In all probability, they were looking for the best ways to defeat their enemies, and this one sect of ants seemed to have it down to a science.

This one group of ants could not be stopped, and they were spreading so fast that they estimated this sect would take over the mass majority of the various types of ants that existed in as little time as the next decade. It was not their size or numbers that made these ants so powerful and unstoppable; instead it was their willingness to sacrifice themselves for the betterment of the colony. One of the chief battle tactics that ensured their success entailed injecting a very poisonous liquid into a few ants over and over again until they became several times larger than all the other ants. These ants would then sacrifice themselves by marching into the middle of the battle-field and exploding this fluid, killing themselves and every ant in the vicinity, friend or foe.[116]

Does this tactic sound familiar? I don't know what the military learned from this, but I realized that sometimes you have to sacrifice and risk it all in order to get it all.

There's No Better Time than the Present

There is an old Chinese proverb that says that the best time to plant a tree was twenty years ago and the second best time is now. When you have decided to take actions that are in support of what you want and have chosen to do this in a way that will manifest it, the next step is to actually take that action. Anything short of just start-ing where you are and taking action is just an excuse, which sends us back up the page to reexplore the section on fear. Most people will stop and focus on all the things that are missing that they need to have in place in order to start a new project, but you just have to start. Remember, focusing on what you don't want causes more of that to show up. So, the first step to getting going is to take the first step and get going. Someone once said that you don't have to be great to start but you at least have to start in order to be great. You have to start where you are and go from there.

The founder of J.C. Penney (James Cash Penney) didn't start his business until he was fifty-six years old.[117] J.C. Penney was born near Hamilton, Missouri, on the sixteenth of September in 1875. At age fifty-six, he came out of an insane asylum and started J.C. Penney. He opened his first store, Golden Rule Store, in the mining town of Kemmerer, Wyoming, in 1902. He changed the store name to the J.C. Penney Co., Inc in 1913. When he retired in 1946, more than 1,600 J.C. Penney stores were in business. At his death in 1971, Pen-ney was ninety-five and left a 1,660-store empire.[118] Do you think he had mastered this truth when he decided to take action regardless of where he was in his life? This story, and others like it, teaches us that the journey of a thousand miles begins with the commitment to take action by taking the first step.

The secret of our success is found in our daily agenda, so you must start by taking the right actions at the right time, and everything else will take care of itself. The easiest way to take the right actions initially is to focus on what's most important first. Remember, a little thing can keep a big thing from happening. A little pebble can hold a boulder in place. You must remember that nothing happens until you take action and that your dreams don't work unless you do! In this instant society, where we have become accustomed to having the things that we want at the snap of our fingers; we have lost value in the process. With the advent of the microwave, fast food, and the instant, just-add-water meals, we have lost the value for the time that it takes to prepare the things that are essential to our existence. If we still had to make everything from scratch, I truly believe that people would appreciate what they were creating, so much so it would reduce, perhaps even totally eliminate, wastefulness, and the health benefits would be immeasurable. This type of instant, something-for-nothing era that we live in transfers into all aspects of our society, including our personal success. Most people are either not willing to go through the refining process that goes into developing yourself personally to achieve the things that they desire or they don't have the patience to see it through. Just like our food analogy, if success is instant, like your mashed potatoes, how will you ever know what the ingredients that go into it are? You see, if you don't know the ingredients, you won't know how to replicate it if you ever have the need to repeat it. This is the reason why quick success is not success at all because it is short lived and can't be maintained or repeated.

Below is a popular joke that illustrates this attitude of something for nothing.

A guy asked God, "God, what is a million years to you?" God replied, "My son, it's like one second in your time." The guy then asked God, "What is a million dollars to you?" God replied, "My son, a million dollars to me is like one penny to you." The guy thought for a few seconds and then asked God, "God, can I have one of your pennies?" God replied and said, "Sure, my son, in just one second."

—Anonymous

Champions don't become champions in the ring; they are merely recognized there."

—Anonymous

If you have worked the rest of this process and have already identified what you want, developed beliefs that support getting it, put together a game plan for its achievement, and created visualizations and affirmations in support of it, this step should come with great ease. The first logical action to take is to work your life plan at least twice a day. The second set of actions to take is to work the game plan established in truth number three in which you created a road map of activities that send you in the direction of your goal. This eliminates the guesswork. It also gives you the clarity necessary to know the appropriate action at all times. The knowledge that everything you are working is in support of what you desire gives you the strength required to overcome all of the fears associated with starting anything new. Fundamentally, if you want to have what someone else has, then you must do what he or she did to get it. And the opposite is true as well. If you want to have what no one else has, you have to do what no one else is doing. The first of these is accomplished by finding someone who already is where you want to be and doing what he or she does. Develop a mentoring relationship with this person, and if this is not possible, then develop a pretend (remember the example about children) mentoring relationship with him or her. Study everything you can about him or her and follow the instructions that he or she has given in their interviews and writings, just as if they were being handed directly to you.

Hopefully you notice that all of the highest actions that you can take include involving other people in your plans. The reason is for every person you add to your action plan, you multiply the acceleration of its accomplishment. John D. Rockefeller once said that he would rather earn 1 percent of one hundred people's efforts than 100 percent of his own.[119] This is especially true if your vision is a grand one. You will find that the bigger your dreams, the bigger your team will need to be in order to accomplish them. This idea of team building to accomplish one's goals is not a new one but is probably the most rewarding aspect of accomplishing your vision. King Solomon, the wisest man in history, whose gold reserves alone would be worth nearly a trillion dollars today, in the book of Proverbs, reveals his strategies for knowledge, wealth, and personal success.

Solomon was born the son of a king and was to be the king of Israel. In this book, he asked God for the wisdom to rule over his people because he was afraid when it was his time to reign, he would not be prepared. It is said that his wisdom created his wealth, and kings and queens from all over sought his advice. His advice on this matter was some of the best advice ever given. He understood that to accomplish anything of significance, it was important to involve other people. This is what he called his accelerator for people who wanted to achieve success beyond their dreams.

> First, gain a clear and concise vision of what you want to achieve.
> Second, put together a detailed road map to achieve that vision.
> Third, always give your vision hope for achieving the goal.
> Fourth, learn to recruit and use partners.[120]

Does any of this sound familiar? Reread it again and see how many of the seven truths you count in these four short lines. Other statements he made in the Bible on this subject are:

> Two are better than one.
>
> Ecclesiastes 4:9–12[121]

> Where there is no counsel the people fall.
>
> Proverbs 11:14[122]

In a multitude of counselors there is safety.

Proverbs 11:14[123]

Without consultation, plans are frustrated, but with many counselors they succeed.

Proverbs 15:22[124]

Whether you are an avid reader and believer of the Bible or not, you
can't deny the wisdom in these writings. Building a team of people
to assist you in your vision is the quickest and most fulfilling way
to accomplish anything of a sizeable measure. This whole concept
of team building was first introduced to me in my network marketing days. Prior to this experience, I had always assembled people to
be a part of whatever vision I had but never in the very calculated
and intentional way that I did while building my network marketing team. I learned that it was one thing to get a bunch of people
together and quite another to unite them around a common goal that
benefited everyone. This is what is meant by building a team that is
as mutually beneficial to the people, supporting the vision, as it is to
the person that has the vision. In order to do great things, you have
to attract people who see what you see and also see that by assist-
ing you in your dreams, they get the automatic benefits of achieving their dreams at the same time. This is the only way a volunteer
organization can function and sustain growth. You must cultivate a
win-win relationship with your team of counselors and partners in
order for it to be truly a venture that has no chance of failing. You
do this by finding people who have goals that are in alignment with
yours and can exist inside of the vision you hold. Always remember that there are no accidents, and every person that you come in
contact with has the potential of playing a role in the attainment of
your vision. As the visionary, your job is to find a way to help each
member of your team achieve his or her goals that are all smaller
parts of your grander goal. Do you see how this process works and
coincides with all that you have read in this chapter? Again, in this
team format, you have learned how to apply this truth at its highest

level. By helping others achieve what they want, you automatically, by default, get the things you want. This may sound just like another one of those sayings, but do you see the implications of this business model? Everyone gets what he or she wants from a situation that provides an opportunity for you to get what you want because you had the vision to create this alliance of benefits for you and all those involved. This is the way our network marketing business worked, and I loved it. All I had to do was help enough people achieve what they were after and I would achieve what I was after. This lesson was one that I learned well, and I was great at it. I excelled at team building in every way, and it's that experience that I credit much of the purpose behind what's being created here.

Getting in the Game

Getting in the game of life requires that you take the actions that support the things you desire. By not taking action, you can very easily find yourself regretting that you didn't follow your heart's desire. This is what happens for those who know what they want but never take the actions necessary for its accomplishment. You have to be willing to take the risk associated with living your dreams. It is much better to have tried and failed than to have failed without even trying. I read a quote by Theodore Roosevelt that made this point so vividly that I typed it up and put it on my wall as a reminder of why I should take action. I repeat it here in the hope that it does the same for you.

> It is not the critic who counts, not the man who points out how the strong man stumbled, or where the doer of deeds could have done them better. The credit belongs to the man who is actually in the arena; whose face is marred by dust and sweat and blood; who strives valiantly; who errs and comes short again and again; who knows the great enthusiasms, the great devotions, and spends himself in a worthy cause; who, at best, knows in the end the triumph of high achievement; and who, at the worst, if he fails, at least fails

while daring greatly, so that his place shall never be with those cold and timid souls who know neither victory nor defeat. [125]

—President Theodore Roosevelt

This excerpt from one of Theodore Roosevelt's speeches reminds us who the real victors are in this time where so much power is given to the pundits who sit back, judge, analyze, and reanalyze others in the arena of life striving and struggling to accomplish their dreams. Those who achieve their own level of greatness all come to the realization that you exchange your entire existence for the things that you do. In other words, be certain that the things or purposes you give or devote your life to are worth it because you are exchanging your life for the different activities you spend your time doing. The thirteenth-century poet Mevlana Jalalal-Din Rumi said, "When you are dead, seek for your resting place not in the earth, but in the hearts of Men."[126] Live your life with purpose!

Truth number six requires that you take the actions required by all of the truths that came before it. However, truth number seven requires you to go ahead and choose to *be* in advance before you *do* the things that are required in order for you to *have* the things that you desire. Truth number seven states you must be thankful in advance for that which has not been created as of yet. Can you see how the application of these proper actions goes hand and hand with this truth? It is for this reason that truth number six precedes truth number seven and represents the prelude to the final, and normally the most difficult, truth to apply. However, the six other truths leading up to this final one have simplified this process, thus making this truth doable for those who have completed the ones before it.

Truth #7

You must be thankful in advance for
that which has not happened yet.

- Application: You must demonstrate faith by living as if what you seek already is. Being thankful in advance for that which has not happened yet is how you demonstrate faith.

- Explanation: By applying each of the six previous truths, you have summoned up the small portions of faith that are required for each truth, but this final truth only requires that you now live with the full expectation that what you seek is now here.

- Manifesting Principle: In the first truth, you were asked to begin with the end in mind; the manifesting principle of this truth asks you to go ahead and live it. Display the attitude now that you would carry if what you are now choosing were already so. Work your goals as if the ones you currently seek have already been obtained. Live from the vision that you hold in your mind, speak as if what you seek is already so, act as if you are already who you seek to be, and it will be so! Being thankful in advance for that which has not happened yet is faith.

These truths used together will design your life plan
for manifesting:

*Truth #1: The first step to getting what you want is to
identify what it is that you want.*

*Truth #2: You must develop beliefs that are in support of
your getting what you want.*

*Truth #3: You must set goals that are in support of what
you want.*

*Truth #4: You must think thoughts that are in support
of what you want.*

*Truth #5: You must speak words that are in support of
what you want.*

*Truth #6: You must take actions that are in support of
what you want.*

*Truth #7: You must be thankful in advance for that
which has not happened yet.*

Every aspect of the proceeding truths prepared you for and asked
you to exercise this truth as part of the process of developing and
defining your life plan. Therefore each truth that came before this
one asks you to apply a small portion of what this last truth will
require you to commit to. The defining of each of the other seven
truths has led you to the edge of the mountain now it's your faith
that will allow you to take the plunge into the uncharted territories
of your life not yet lived. True faith requires that you proceed forward even in the absence of the presence of proof that what you are
now walking in is so or even possible for that matter.

Faith is the starting point of all accumulation of miracles.

—Napoleon Hill[127]

Defining Faith

What is faith to you? Most people describe faith as their belief in something that there is no evidence to indicate that it is so or that it has the potential to be. Others have defined it as follows:

- Faith is a strong belief in a supernatural power or powers that control human destiny.

- Faith is complete confidence in a person or plan.

- Faith is loyalty or allegiance to a cause or person.

- Faith is confident belief in the truth, value, or trustworthiness of a person, an idea, or a thing.

- Faith is the belief that does not rest on logical proof or material evidence.

- Faith is what you have when the presence or absence of empirical evidence doesn't matter.

Regardless of which of these definitions resonate with you or if you have a totally different definition, the question is do you see how that definition coincides with the life plan that you have designed through this process? Developing trust in yourself and the life plan that you have designed via these seven truths will afford you the belief that will eventually transfer into faith. This is what this chapter is designed to teach you. It's about faith in action. Many people say that they have faith, but they do nothing that would give them a chance to exercise it. If you have dreams and say that you have faith but you are not working toward them, then your dream is already dead alongside your faith.

Faith in Action

There are two things that present themselves as obstacles in this process of living from your faith. The first is that most people only live out of faith when they absolutely have no other choice. When everything else has failed them, all possible options have been expired, and there is nothing else left, people tend to have their first real experience with faith. It's only when we have no choice that we choose to exercise our highest choice. I will be the first to admit that this is how I have usually experienced faith in action in my life. I can't count the times that I absolutely needed nothing short of a miracle to get me out of a situation. Usually, after I had exhausted all other possibilities, something would happen right in the nick of time that was unexpected and beyond my control to bail me out.

One of the biggest examples of this was on my wedding day. I had planned a weeklong celebration commencing a few days prior to my wedding and lasting a few days after. I invited all of my friends and family to vacation with us at the resort where we planned to marry, which was on a beach. We figured we could enjoy our friends and family for a full week and get married in the middle of this weeklong celebration. This was one of the best times of our lives. Having both sides of the family there, many of them meeting for the very first time, it couldn't have been better.

Not long before the festivities, I had closed on a real estate trans-action and made thirty thousand dollars. I set the majority of it aside for this weeklong celebration, the wedding, and our honeymoon.

The day of the wedding, we had plenty to do, including remind-ing all of our guests that we still had a wedding taking place, and they would need to stop partying long enough to participate. We were getting close to the time for the wedding to start and were in the process of taking the wedding pictures with my father and the groomsmen when I noticed that the staff, which was preparing the tables, began to take the tablecloths off the table and stopped deco-rating. When I inquired as to what was happening, they told me that I needed to see the head person in charge. When I made it to his office, he was in a panic. He explained that my bank had reversed all of the charges that I had made on my bank card. And that if I didn't come up with the entire amount of money, including the balances that weren't even currently due, the entire wedding would have to be called off. He further explained that I, many of my family members, and guests, whose rooms I had paid for with that card, would have to immediately check out. I explained to him that there had to be a logical explanation and that I would get on the phone with my bank and fix it. I immediately called my bank, and they informed me that not only had they reversed the charges, but until they collected all of the money that had been paid out of the account, they were freezing my other two accounts that I had with them. When I inquired why all this was happening, they explained that the check that I had deposited almost two weeks earlier and had cleared came back to them as fraudulent and had been written on a bad account. As you can imagine, I became very weak in the knees. I called the gentleman who had given me the check for eighty thousand dollars, of which thirty thousand of it was my cut, fully confident that he would fix this mess and get things straightened out. The question was could he do it before my soon-to-be wife found out, who was now getting her hair done? I reached him at his office, and to make a long story short, he basically told me that he didn't know what I was talking about, that he didn't owe me any money, and not to call him again. Now, at this time, I didn't know whether to stay and get married or go to Atlanta and most likely end up in jail. As I called around to other people that knew him, I began to hear stories that affirmed this wasn't the first time he had mistreated someone this way. Thus, I realized he wasn't going to be an option for fixing this problem. I called everyone I could think of, and no one could help me. Most of the people that I knew were there on the beach somewhere without their cell phones. At this point, I knew nothing else that I could do, so I just sat there in disbelief. It was all falling apart right in front of me, and there was nothing I could do about it. I remember thinking that things would work out. If I just didn't panic and remained faithful, what I was going through would pass and I would be okay. Somehow, the word began to circulate as one friend or family member passed on to the next what was happening and why the wedding didn't look like it was going to start on time. As I went to my brothers and other people, attempting to see if I could borrow money, the deadline the resort had given me was approaching. So I headed back toward the event coordinator's office to ask for an extension or whether he would accept a smaller amount than he had asked for. Just before I reached the office, a friend of mine came rushing in, dripping with sweat, with a fist full of credit cards with little notes taped on the back that had the pin number and the amount of money that I could use from each card. My friends and family had found one another on the beach and all chipped in. When it was all added up, it was just the amount I needed. Thankfully the wedding and the rest of the week went on as planned. As a side note, I never got my money and that guy who wrote me the bogus check was already wanted by the FBI for the same or similar types of fraudulent transactions, so he ended up in jail.

This is just one example of the many times that my faith was the only thing that pulled me through. I'm certain that no one would like to endure what I did simply to see faith at work. There has to be an easier way for faith to show up and work miracles in your life. And this is exactly what this truth is designed to teach you to achieve.

I would like to add that it is very easy to confuse beliefs with faith and possibly miss the opportunity to apply this truth. Fortunately, this can be remedied by simply comparing the two to understand how they differ in application.

Belief Versus Faith

- *Beliefs* are impressions, opinions, or feelings one holds as true while *faith* is complete confidence or allegiance to something or someone without logical proof.

- *Belief* relates most to knowledge and understanding; *faith* relates mostly to hope and trust.

- *Belief* may or may not imply that the believer is certain, whereas *faith* implies a level of assurance that approaches certainty.

- *Belief* requires that you only believe; *faith* requires you to act upon that belief.

> We must walk consciously only part way toward our goal and then leap in the dark to our success.
>
> —Henry David Thoreau[128]

When you consider these differences, it's easy to see how one requires you to go beyond your normal comfort zone and stretch into newer dimensions of belief that exceed your normal capacity to embrace. So how do you go beyond the limitations of your beliefs to exercising this tool called faith without being in a crisis to do so? You must first understand that beliefs lead to knowing, and knowing does not follow experience; it produces it. This can be a difficult process to follow, but the quickest way to experience something that you have yet to live is by acting as if you have already done it. You must take yourself there mentally first by asking, "If I had my heart's desire, how would I behave, what would I say or believe, and more importantly, how would I feel?" This is how you transform belief into faith. You must be that which you desire. In turn, you are demonstrating to the universe the faith (knowing) that it is so, and the universe will manifest the experience into your reality. Designing your wedding dress and setting a date before you find your fiancé is an example of faith in action. Test-driving your dream car, leaving a deposit, and an expected pick up date without a known means of acquiring it is faith in action. Let me assure you, I'm not talking about blind, naive faith, even though that kind works too, but I'm talking about the type of faith that says, "I have done all that I can do, and I'm turning the rest over to my faith." This type of action requires you to walk up to the edge of belief, jump right off, and develop wings on the way down. Now, I know that some people will say, "You must be out of your mind to think that I would take a blind leap into the unknown all in the name of having faith." I'm not proposing anything that radical.

However, what this chapter is going to ask you to do will require you to literally be out of your mind, and your body too, for that matter. But it won't be a blind leap.

> Thou hast been faithful over a few things, I will make thee ruler over many things.
>
> Matthew 25:21[129]

As airy fairy as most people's thoughts are when it comes to this topic of faith, it's not as abstract a subject as you may think. There is a process for developing and applying faith that is very scientific in nature. The part that requires you to face the unknown can be eliminated by a very simple exercise that's designed to teach you how to be the things to get what you seek versus doing the things required. Have you ever wondered why we are called human beings and not human doings? Speaking in Ebonics, we are what we *be* and not what we *do*. It is for this reason if you can name anything that you would like to be (which is the end result) instead of what you would have to do (which is the beginning), you can become it in this very instant.

Think about anyone who is where you want to be or whom you look up to. What are their characteristics? Are they humble, excited, happy, loving, peaceful, healthy, or joyful? Frankly, in the end, a life filled with these emotions and characteristics is what we're all after. You may say, "No, that's not what I want. What I want is to be super rich." But ask yourself, do you want to be rich, or do you want to have the things that being rich afford you? If you stop and honestly reflect upon this question, you will realize that if you were super rich but didn't have any of the before-mentioned characteristics, all your things wouldn't even matter. In essence, most people are after the feelings and characteristics associated with being rich. Ask yourself how you think it feels to be rich. What characteristics do you associate with being rich? What would you be more of? Would you be more approachable, friendly, easy going, sincere, or anything else? Take the time to answer this question. Your answers may shock you.

THE 7 TRUTHS OF LIFE

For me, I thought being rich would make me more confident, more assured of my future, humble, fulfilled, joyful, giving, and even more forgiving. After you take a look at each of your descriptions, no matter what you wrote down, realize you have the ability to be any or all of these things in the blink of an eye. Here's the greatest secret of all times: you don't have to do anything to be any of these things that you have named. You are just one thought away, just one decision, from being any of these things. You can decide to be honest right this very second; you can decide to be humble, peaceful, friendly, excited, or anything else. Again, this is why we are human beings versus human doings; it's not about what we do that determines who we are; it's all about what we are being. Decide who you would be if you already had the things that you desire by defining the feeling you would have and the characteristics you would possess. Begin to live those characteristics now and you will begin to experience being that which you desire. Remember, this is an exercise in faith. You have to take the steps to go forth and believe, work, think, speak, and act as if what you seek already is. This actual walking in your faith is the manifesting principle for truth number seven.

Infinite patience produces immediate results.

—Dr. Helen Schucman[130]

Exercise in Faith

I used to teach a leadership class in which I would ask people to try this exercise, not as an experiment in faith but as a practical approach toward experiencing what they desired by living its characteristics. It was designed to teach the participants that being a leader, or anything else, for that matter, was just a state of mind. Each participant was asked to identify a leader, or multiple leaders, who represented the type of leader he or she would like to be. After they identified those people, they were then asked to list the characteristics that these leaders had that they would like to see present in themselves.

They would often list things like humble, sincere, hardworking, honest, and so on. I would then ask them to select one characteristic on the list that they could not decide to be that very instant. They would look at their list and say, "There isn't any that can't be done right away." They could decide to be humble, sincere, honest, and hardworking that very second and never change their minds about it again. It became apparent to all that they could instantly become a leader by adopting all of the characteristics of the leaders they had chosen. This process is the exact same when choosing the characteristics that you foresee your future self being. Decide to live from those characteristics and choose nothing else. This acting it out brings it about, and this is manifesting.

> Can you imagine having to grow the trees versus just planting the seeds?
>
> —Anonymous

Letting Go and Letting God

When it comes to letting go and letting God, there are two different extreme schools of thought as to how to apply this to your life and make it work as part of your manifesting process. The first extreme encompasses individuals who say things such as, "I will do this or that if God's willing," or "I guess I will get what I'm after if it's what God wants for me." Here's the thing: God is willing, and he wants for you what you want for you. The second extreme are the individuals who believe that letting go and letting God is the lazy person's way of not taking responsibility for the outcomes of his life; they're the I-will-make-it-happen people. This is the person who says, "If it's going to be, it's up to me." Both extremes are unhealthy and are hampering their ability to manifest. These two extremes have forgotten that there's a balance between them. After you have done all that you can do, by letting go and letting God, you demonstrate that you have faith in your creator and in your contributions toward what's being created. Whereas the person of the first extreme may have heard the saying, "Let go and let God" and believed it sounded good, nonetheless, their application of this truth was faulty, for true faith requires you to believe enough to move forward and take actions toward what you desire. This is drastically different from I will do or receive something if God is willing or wants me too. There was a saying that they used to say in my prior network marketing company that "God ain't going to steer no parked car." In other words, you have got to do your part before you ask God to do his. Or put another way, you have to do the possible before you can expect the impossible. On the flip side, the person who embraces the other extreme that he or she must do everything robs him or herself of the magic that comes from having faith and allowing the universe to move on his or her behalf. I too have been guilty of this extreme. Time and again, I've tried to do it all myself until I reached the point that I couldn't contribute anything else. It's only then that I've admitted that the problem was beyond my control and must be handled by something other than myself. These are the two basic extremes: the person who tries to do it all without the support of the universe and the person who wants God to do it all. Invariably, you must strike a balance between your contributing effort toward accomplishing your goal and having faith that what you want is already so. It's what I call meeting the universe halfway. It's about handling everything that's in your control and letting God handle everything that's not.

> By faith we understand that the universe was formed at God's command, so that what is seen was not made out of what was visible.
>
> Hebrews 11:3[131]

The first time I used this entire method for manifesting, I decided what I wanted, checked my attitude, set my goals, did my visualizations and affirmations, took the actions, and then let God do the rest. Without fail, when I truly let go and let God, the magic happened.

The story of Peter Daniels is an example of a life lived by striking the balance, between letting go and letting God and making it happen.

Peter Daniels never went to college, or even passed a grade, for that matter. It was thought that he had brain damage. A concerned teacher took interest in Peter but later came back to say there was no hope for him, that he was just plain stupid. At the age of twenty-six years old, he couldn't read or write.

In 1959, he heard Billy Graham speak during a crusade and realized that he could do anything and was equal to anyone. He said that evening God gave him a dream to see how much money one human being could give away in a lifetime.

He went out and bought three dictionaries and walked around pointing at words and asking people what they meant. Once he was able to read, he read two thousand biographies.

Astoundingly, he went from being completely illiterate at age twenty-six to owning the only privately owned gold and silver bullion bank in the entire world. In fact, it is the only corporation in the world that has its own currency.

Two companies paid him a million dollars for advice. One of those companies only received ten minutes worth of advice and made 120 million dollars from it. Both Peter Daniels and his son are ranked within the top 10 percent of advisors in the entire world.

Daniels's goal now is to change the world for the next three hundred years, just like Rodger Bannister, Gandhi, and Henry Ford.[132]

If you revisit the definition of faith, you would have to say that Peter Daniels's life is a great example of what having faith truly means.

Every aspect of the six previous truths prepared you for and asked you to exercise faith. The first truth asked you to predetermine what you would choose to have for yourself by beginning with the end in mind. This only requires you to exercise a small amount of faith. Nevertheless, to see what you want without any evidence that you will receive it requires faith. The second truth asked that you believe that you can achieve what you want, which requires a little additional faith. The third truth asked that you go ahead and make plans and set goals to get what you want, which requires more faith since you're actually taking action. Again, this is all still being done absent of proof that what you seek is within your grasp. The fourth, fifth, and sixth truths ask that you think thoughts, speak words, and take actions that claim you already have what you're after, and this is faith in action. So as you can see, you have been applying small amounts of faith throughout each step of the six truths. Now, the seventh truth requires you to apply them all at the same time. Since you've been exercising small bits of faith throughout this process, taking this next step should just be the natural consequence of a life plan well designed and executed. This is applied faith, which is truth number seven and its manifesting principle.

Chapter 8
Pulling It All Together

What You Do Is What You Exchange Your Life For

Choosing your life's work can be a very difficult thing to do for some, whereas for others it comes very naturally. Regardless of the level of difficulty or simplicity, what matters most is taking the time to get this right. Whatever you spend your life doing, you will be exchanging your life for. With so much at stake, you must make sure that what you are doing is worth it.

> You are here to enable the divine Purpose of the universe to unfold.
> That is how important you are!
> —Eckhart Tolle[133]

Taking the time to work these seven truths will help your life's work spell itself out. By taking the time, no matter how long this process takes, you'll put your life on course and give your work meaning. After all, this is your life we're talking about. Don't you deserve a life filled with meaning, passion, and purpose? In the long run, you getting this right will benefit us all.

I believe that we owe it to ourselves and those who depend on us, especially our children, to live the best lives we can. Also, I believe we owe it to one another. Your life well lived benefits you, me, everyone, and everything else on this planet. Through discovering and living your life's purpose, you add to the perfection of the universe and help raise the consciousness of all things. For this reason, I honor our oneness and I honor our individuality.

Mohandas Gandhi once said, "Let us become the change we seek in the world."[134] He was asking us to live our grandest version of our lives by becoming the change we seek in the world. The change we seek is found in what we desire, for, as we now know, all change is initiated by desire.

I created the mantra for myself that I would not complain about something that I could do something about. The things that we complain about are the things that we would like to change, and this text is designed to teach you how to become that change in your personal life. Ultimately, this is all that life asks of you.

All of us have our unique missions embedded within us. Awakening and fulfilling that mission is our individual contribution to the body of humanity of which we're all a part. Do you see how each of us makes up the whole of us? As each of us reaches the grandest version of ourselves, so does the whole of us. Knowing this alone should give your life a new purpose that's larger than the one you identified through these seven truths.

George Bernard Shaw wrote:

This is the true joy in life—the being used for a purpose recognized by yourself as a mighty one. The being a force of nature, instead of a feverish, selfish little clod of ailments, and grievances; complaining that the world will not devote itself to making you happy. I am of the opinion that my life belongs to the whole community, and as long as I live, it is my privilege to do for it whatever I can. I want to be thoroughly used up when I die-for the harder I work, the more I live. I rejoice in life for its own sake. Life is no "brief candle" to me; it is a sort of splendid torch, which I have got hold of for the moment, and I want to make it burn as brightly as possible before handing it on to future generations.[135]

We must commit ourselves to living the largest, grandest, version of ourselves we can conceive. The solutions to the obstacles presented in this book will ensure that this is accomplished by all that seek to apply the truths contained within these pages.

> If you are not living on the edge then you are taking up to much room.
>
> —Peter J. Daniels[136]

The writing of this book is my attempt at contributing the best that I have to offer the world. As I worked through all of the many road-blocks that kept me from the manifestation of this book, which I consider to be my life's purpose, I now realize that it was me that was holding me back. Every person, situation, or circumstance that I felt was the cause of my not living my purpose was really my choosing to be less than what I knew was possible for myself. The mistake I made was to stop being me. I stopped living my life on my own terms in an effort to blend in. All of my life I felt alone, as if I were a one-man show and there was no one who thought the things that I thought or wanted the things that I wanted. So I stopped creating and started assimilating. I wanted to be more like everyone else instead of living at my highest level. When I was on purpose and living what I felt was the highest version of my life I often accomplished every goal that I set out to. Still, it was a lonely place. I felt like there was no one else there but me. I didn't realize it was my attitude and belief that I was alone that was manifesting loneliness into my reality. Like so many, in an attempt to please more people, I began more and more to downplay myself, even to my own detriment, so that those around me wouldn't feel intimidated. This is why my success has always had limits. Even in my worst self-defeating times, I would still always exceed everyone's expectations of me. Then, fearfully, I would cut it off to make certain that I didn't exceed my own. I then read the fol-lowing quote written by Marianne Williamson, and it freed me from this self-limiting behavior. I repeat it here in hopes that it will free anyone else suffering from this self defeating mentality.

Our deepest fear is not that we are inadequate. Our deepest fear is that we are powerful beyond measure. It is our light, not our darkness, that most frightens us. We ask ourselves, who am I to be brilliant, gorgeous, talented and fabulous? Actually, who are you not to be? You are a child of God. Your playing small doesn't serve the world. There is nothing enlightened about shrinking so other people won't feel insecure around you. We are born to make manifest the glory of God that is within us. It's not just in some of us; it's in everyone. And as we let our own light shine, we un-consciously give other people permission to do the same. As we feel liberated from our own fear, our presence automatically liberates others.

—Marianne Williamson[137]

The Bigger Implication

We are all connected. We aren't just connected to one another, but to everything that exists. In the documentary *The Eleventh Hour,* presented by Leonardo DiCaprio, over 150 scientists from all over the world were commissioned to examine the impact we are making on our ecosystem and nature as a whole.[138] The one thing the experts discovered that they unanimously agreed upon was there is no separation and everything is connected. What we do to nature that harms it also harms us.

Spirituality is the only answer to the problems that plague the world.

—Anonymous[139]

I remember watching something disturbing on the news and saying to myself, "If something like that happened to someone close to me, I would go crazy and most likely lose it," not realizing that it was happening to someone close to me. In essence, whatever happens to one of us happens to all of us. For this reason, when we see something that is not a representation of the highest good, we must all demand change. Not just for the sake of a few, but for the sake of us all.

Shifting your consciousness to the realization that we're all connected will broaden your scope of responsibility past the limited
view of just your immediate family. The things that diminish one of
us diminish all of us, and the absence of this inclusive truth in our
collective awareness allows injustices to happen to thousands and
even millions of others while the rest of us feel unaffected. If we
begin to see ourselves as connected to everyone and everything, we
will immediately begin to heal the ills of this world.

I often tell people that if your kids have everything and my kids
have nothing, no matter how well I raise them, the odds are great
that eventually they will try to take what your kids have and vice
versa. Obviously I don't mean this literally, but this is where the
mass majority of our conflicts emerge. If we don't learn to share our
resources and continue down this path of the haves desiring to have
more and more while the have-nots are forced to live with fewer and
fewer resources, then this prediction will become an expanding reality. Each of us has the ability to begin to reverse this process by being
the change that we seek.

Demand change, even if it's a large one. Be the change even if
it's a small one. I remember noticing many years ago that my local
grocery store had switched to one of those self-scan systems that one
person could monitor while eight people checked out at the exact
same time. I remember thinking to myself this one change was a
great convenience for the customers and I'm certain very cost effective for the storeowner, but the larger implication was that at least
fifteen young people had lost a job opportunity. Not only were seven
or eight cashier jobs probably lost but another seven or eight gro-
cery-bagging jobs as well. Both of these opportunities were great
starter jobs for young people, and they now were eliminated in the
name of more profits for the grocery storeowner. Now, perhaps the
storeowner wasn't considering this when he or she was looking at
all of the benefits of this type of system, but this is the reality of the
matter. I made a decision that very moment that I would never use
that self-scanner, no matter how crowded the regular lines were. You
may say that's a really small thing to do, but if you multiply those fif-

teen lost jobs by the amount of self-scanners that are now in almost every grocery store in America, you can begin to see the impact. By not using them and encouraging other people not to, I hope to show people the damage that can occur with something so simple. Our youth now have a few thousand jobs less to keep them busy, out of trouble, and able to earn money. This is just one small example of being the change that you seek. Take the time to look for your causes, large or small, and inspire someone else to do the same.

Which Are You?

There are two kinds of people on earth today
Just two kinds of people, no more, I say
Not the sinner and saint, for 'tis well understood
The good are half bad, and the bad are half good
Not the rich and the poor, for to count someone's wealth
You must first know the state of their conscience and health.
Not the humble and proud, for you see it's like this,
The humble are proud, and the proud are remiss.
Not the happy and sad, for the swift flying years
Bring each one their laughter and each one their tears.
No, the two kinds of people on earth I mean,
Are the people who lift and the people who lean.
Wherever you go, you will find the world's masses
Are always divided in just these two classes.
And oddly enough you will find too, I mean,
There are just a few lifters and many who lean.
In which class are you? Are you easing the load,
Of overtaxed lifters who toil down the road?
Or are you a leaner, who lets the other bear
Your portion of labor and worry and care?

—Ella Wheeler Wilcox[140]

Change in Consciousness

This change in consciousness is already happening. One of the clearest examples of this is the 2008 presidential election. Nearly everyone knew he or she wanted change on an individual level, but it wasn't until Barack Obama stepped on the scene and announced that he was going to make the change that it became obvious just how many people sought the same thing. The consciousness of change was already here. Barack Obama just happened to be the person who stepped up and decided to embrace it and be its representative. Some might even say that he caused this change in consciousness by being so committed to change on the large scale that he represents. He instantly became the leader of this shift in consciousness. But the real question is which one came first, the collective consciousness desiring change or the person who would lead the movement for change?

During the civil rights movement, millions of people sought change, and this created the consciousness of change. And like Barack, a person emerged as the leader or representative of that shift in consciousness, Dr. Martin Luther King Jr. Since the civil rights movement is recent history, it's easy for us to see how this consciousness of change already existed and how many people were already seeking it. Most of the first representatives of this movement were creating this change in consciousness many years before the leader was even born. Is there anyone who would argue that what Dr. Martin Luther King Jr. accomplished within the short thirty-nine years he was on this earth was not his purpose for being on this planet? Do you ever hear people saying that he would have made a much better anything other than what he was? Everything about him—the timing of his birth, his parents, exposure to the church, education, and the oratory skills required to become a Baptist preacher—prepared him to assume the position that fulfilled his destiny. As you think about this and reflect on all that has been shared within the pages of this book, do you think any of this is an accident? Clearly, one can recognize that it was the unity of collective consciousness that gave birth to a leader whose life's mission was to shine light on the injustice of discrimination based on race, religion, sexual orientation, nationality, and, perhaps even more profound, the importance of solving humanity's conflicts peacefully. Even at a slight glance, you can clearly see how all of the pieces to this puzzle that represents Dr. Martin Luther King's life and the collective consciousness for change fit together perfectly to form the manifestation that we saw represented in this historic chain of events.

Now, let's take a look at the current example of group consciousness and its call for change. Just as in the movement with Dr. Martin Luther King, Jr., everything about President Barack Obama has prepared him to represent the change the mass majority of people are obviously seeking worldwide. All of the pieces of his life aligned perfectly so he would be the person and this would be the time. The son of a biracial couple, raised by a single mother, part of his childhood spent abroad, his education and expertise in constitutional law, his community service efforts, and political career are all a part of his life experiences that have clearly molded him to be the perfect person to represent the change that a large portion of the entire world desires. Only the divine intelligence of the universe can align events so perfectly, thus preparing him to be the person with the appropriate background, skills, and message, for this time.

Creating a New World

Can you imagine a world where everyone's basic needs are being met and everyone is granted the opportunity to achieve his or her desires by following these natural laws? I know this type of outcome sounds naïve, and if you let the media guide your thinking, then you may even consider this impossible. Yet this type of consciousness already exists in other parts of the world, and these types of results are happening in various places in the world.

I remember watching an Oprah show about a mother in Iceland that blew me away. It was so incredible to learn that in Iceland the

women are allowed to stay home on maternity leave with their new-
born children for nine months after giving birth and are paid by the
government and their employers.[141] The other thing that amazed me
which was not part of the story line of the show was that I noticed that
some of the mothers left their babies in their strollers parked outside
of the stores while they went shopping.[142] This was absolutely shock-
ing to me. They can do this because there is almost no crime at all.[143]
I was simply astonished, so much so that I decided to research Iceland
further to discover the catalyst to creating the type of collective consciousness that allows people to live in harmony this way. What I found
is exactly what's being described here in this last chapter.

The first thing that I learned was that Iceland topped the latest
table of the United Nations Development Programme's (UNDP)
Human Development Index rankings.[144] This means that as a society
and as an economy, in terms of wealth, health, and education, they
are the champions of the world. As I did my research, I found that
Iceland has dark winters and far from tropical summers. With such
dreary weather, I wondered if Icelanders were happy. From what I
discovered, in so far as one can reliably measure such things, they are.
According to an academic study reported in the *Guardian* in 2006,
Icelanders are the happiest people on earth.[145] Interestingly, Iceland
has the sixth highest GDP per capita in the world; Icelanders read
more books per capita than any other citizenry in the world; the life
expectancy for men is the highest in the world and not far behind
for women; it's the only country in NATO with no armed forces
(they were banned seven hundred years ago); it has the highest ratio
of mobile telephones to population, the fastest expanding banking
system in the world, a rocketing export business market, crystal-pure
air, and clean geothermal energy delivered to all Icelandic house-
holds, straight from the earth's volcanic bowels.[146]

Certainly, you would think, based on what you have read so
far, that this place must be make-believe and doesn't exist. But it
does, and they're not doing anything that we can't do. It's just that
their value system places a premium on what's most beneficial for all
versus what's best for the few.[147] This is not just the mantra of the

people; it's also the mantra of the government. Their government is of the people, by the people, and for the people instead of, like most industrialized nations, only for special interest groups. For instance, in the earlier example, I touched upon the fact that the state gives women nine months fully paid maternity leave. However, I neglected to mention that this paid leave may be split between the mother and the father as they so please. Thus, employers realize that the men they hire are just as likely to take time off to look after their newborns as the women.[148] Furthermore, Iceland has exceptionally low personal and corporate tax rates; they receive not just free, top-class education but free top-class health care with private medicine being limited in Iceland to mainly luxury procedures, such as cosmetic surgery.[149] Thus, they meet the basic needs of everyone and provide an unlimited opportunity for those who seek more. These are just a few examples of the beneficial quality of life that has emerged from the collective thought process of the people of Iceland.

Iceland is just one of several countries that have gotten it right and are headed in the direction that will heal our world. Do your own research and see how others have been able to return our world back to the natural balance that we spoke of earlier in this book. Then truly you will discover, as I have, that there's nothing naïve or airy-fairy about the implications or the promise of this book for you personally and for all of us collectively.

Make It Work for You

The application of the information in this book will impact you on many different levels. However, not until you pass this information on will you attain the full benefit of this work. This is how it has worked for me. Although I knew the information conceptually, it wasn't until I taught it here in this book, the accompanying workbook, and lecture series that I actually owned it. This is how the law of reciprocity works. You truly do get what you give, and the more you give, then the more you will experience having. This truth requires action to be realized. Therefore, you will only experience this truth by doing and observing the results. Find ways to share what you have learned here with others and donate at minimum 10 percent of what you create via the application of these seven truths to a charity of your choice or any organization that improves the collective human condition.

All of Life Is a Process of Creation and Creation Is Represented By Change

The adjective for life is change, and all change is fueled by desire. Desire is the currency and catalyst for all that happens. Change is constant, and everything that's alive is always changing from its birth to its never-ending transformation that we call death. Desire is the motivating factor that causes life to propel itself forward, and once you have mastered the process of creation via the application of these seven truths, it's now time to engage in the process of manifestation. Remember, manifestation is the verb meaning to turn thoughts into things, and when you manifest something, you metaphorically reach your hand through the invisible curtain separating the tangible world and pull your desired object into existence.[150]

Now, creation requires a lapse in time while manifestation is not limited by the restraints of time. To manifest is to create with the absence of time. Faithfully applying these seven truths in their highest form moves one from the process of creation to the process of manifestation.

Lets Recap:

Truth #1

- Creation: The first step to getting what you want is to identify what it is that you want.

- Manifestation: Change your wants into desires and your desires into a choosing.

Truth #2

- Creation: You must develop beliefs that are in support of your getting what you want.

- Manifestation: The highest form of a supporting belief is a supporting attitude. Changing from beliefs that support what you want to an attitude that supports it is the quickest way to manifest it.

Truth #3

- Creation: You must set goals that are in support of what you want.

- Manifestation: The highest form of goal setting is when your goals are written in a way that creates a roadmap that leads toward the achievement of them.

Truth# 4

- Creation: You must think thoughts that are in support of what you want.

- Manifestation: You have to create visualizations in your mind of what you would like to manifest into your reality.

Truth #5

- Creation: You must speak words that are in support of what you want.

- Manifestation: You must create affirmations and incantations that speak words that are a reflection of who you are and what you are now choosing to be. An affirmation affirms that which you choose to be true in your life.

Truth #6

- Creation: You must take actions that are in support of what you want.

- Manifestation: To help someone else experience within himself that which you wish to experience in yourself is the highest action that you can take.

Truth #7

- Creation: You must be thankful in advance for that which has not happened yet.

- Manifestation: In the first truth, you were asked to begin with the end in mind; the manifesting principle of this truth asks you to go ahead and live it. Display the attitude now that you would carry if what you are now choosing was already so. Work your goals as if the ones you currently seek have already been obtained. Live from the vision that you hold in your mind, speak as if what you seek was already so, act as if you already are who you are seeking to be, and it will be so!

Every time I reread the seven truths, I'm reminded of one of the most beautiful explanations I've ever read on the process of creation, which solidifies how and why these seven truths work. In a book called *Conversations with God* by Neal Donald Walsh, God speaks and says:

You were created in the likeness and image of God. God is the creator. You are three beings in one—people call it father, son, and Holy Ghost—mind, body, and spirit—superconscious, conscious, and subconscious. Creation is a process that proceeds from these three parts of your body. Put another way, you create at three levels. The tools of creation are thought, word, and deed. All creation begins with thought, proceeds from the father, all creation then moves to word—ask and you shall receive—speak and it shall be done unto you—all creation is fulfilled in deed and the word was made flesh and dwelled among us. That which you think of and thereafter never speak of creates at one level; that which you think of and speak of creates at another level; that which you think, speak, and do becomes manifest in your reality. To think, speak, and do something that you do not believe is impossible.[151]

Use these *Seven Truths of Life* to design and build the life of your choice and then teach someone else to do the same. As you begin to see your grandest vision of life begin to manifest itself, please contact us and let us know of your progress. We would love to use your success to inspire someone else to begin the process of living the highest version of themselves. Re-member (to put back together) the pieces of your puzzle by recognizing the hints and reminders that you set up for yourself before coming here to live out the life that you pre-designed. Do this and experience *your life on your terms, intentionally designed for you by you.*

Happy manifesting,
Senghor Pope

Endnotes

1 Hansen, Mark Victor and Robert G. Allen. The One-Minute Millionaire: The Enlightened Way to Wealth. New York, NY: Harmony Books 2002.

2 Hansen

3 *The Last Samurai.* Dir. Edward Zwick. Perf. Tom Cruise, Ken Watanabe, Billy Connolly, William Atherton, Chad Lindberg. Warner Bros, 2003. DVD. Warner Home Video, May 4, 2004.

4 *Finding Oprah's Roots.* Perf. Oprah Winfrey, Henry Louis Gates Jr. PBS, 2007. PBS Paramount, May 1, 2007.

5 Murphy, Joseph. *The Power of Your Subconscious Mind (First Edition).* Englewood Cliffs NJ: Prentice Hall 1964.

6 Stein, Ben. *How Successful People Win: Using Bunkhouse Logic to Get What You Want in Life.* United States: Hay House, Inc. 1981.

7 Walsch, Neale Donald. *Conversations with God: An Uncommon Dialogue (Book 1).* New York, NY: G.P. Putnam's Sons, 1996.

8 Walsch

9 Walsch

10 Hill, Napoleon. *Think and Grow Rich.* The Ralston Publishing Co. 1954.

11 Dyer, Wayne W., Dr. *Manifest Your Destiny.* New York, NY: HarperCollins Publishing, Inc. 1997.

12 Dyer

13　Scott, Cynthia D., Dennis T. Jaffe and Glenn R. Tobe. *Organizational Vision, Values and Mission: Building the Organization of Tomorrow (1st Edition).* Crisp Learning 1993.

14　Matthew 6:21, The King James Bible.

15　Conwell, Russell H. *Acres of Diamonds.* Temple University 2008. (Accessed November 2008)<http://www.temple.edu/about/Acres_of_Diamonds.htm>

16　Dyer, Wayne W. *You'll See It When You Believe It: The Way to Your Personal Transformation.* New York, NY: HarperCollins Publishers Inc. 1989.

17　Smith, Sydney. Wikiquote Sydney Smith 2008. (Accessed November 24, 2008) http://en.wikiquote.org/wiki/Sydney_Smith

18　Proverbs 16:9, The King James Bible.

19　Canfield, Jack. Jack Canfield's Key to Living the Law of Attraction: A Simple Guide to Creating the Life of Your Dreams. Deerfield Beach, FL: Health Communications, Inc. 2007.

20　Porter, Patrick K. *Awaken the Genius: Mind Technology for the 21ˢᵗ Century.* Virginal Beach, VA: Positive Changes 1993.

21　Napoleon Hill talks about his meeting with Andrew Carnegie. Napoleon Hill. YouTube 2008. (Accessed on November 24, 2008) http://www.youtube.com/watch?v=1GCaEZscfvA&feature=related

22　Hill, Napoleon. *Think and Grow Rich.* New York, NY: Random House Publishing, Inc. 1960.

23　Hill

24　How To Get What You Really Want. Wayne W. Dyer, Deepak Chopra. Public Broadcasting Service. 1998.

25　William, Shakespeare. Hamlet, Prince of Denmark. The Plays and Sonnets of William Shakespeare (Volume Two), Encyclopedia Britannica Great Books of the Western World. Edited by William George Clarke and William Aldis Wright. Chicago, IL: William Benton 1952.

26 Walsch, Neale Donald. *Conversations with God: An Uncommon Dialogue (Book 1)*. New York, NY: G.P. Putnam's Sons, 1996.

27 Dyer, Wayne W. *Living the Wisdom of the Tao: The Complete Tao Te Ching and Affirmations*. United States: Hay House, Inc., 2008.

28 Diamond, John, Dr. *Your Body Doesn't Lie*. New York, NY: Harper & Row Publishers, Inc. 1979.

29 Hawkins, David R. *Power vs. Force: The Hidden Determinants of Human Behavior*. Carlsbad, CA: Hay House, Inc. 1995.

30 Hawkins

31 Hawkins

32 Jefferson, Thomas. (n.d.). Quotes.net 2004–2007t. (Accessed November 25, 2008) http://www.quotes.net/quote/8064

33 Ward, William Arthur. *Fountains of Faith: The Words of William Arthur Ward*. Anderson, SC: Drake House 1970.

34 Sacks, David. *Letter Perfect: The Marvelous History of Our Alphabet From A to Z*. United States: Broadway Books 2003.

35 Sacks

36 Sacks

37 Sacks

38 Scribd. Attitude Is Everything. Scribd Website 2008 (Accessed September, 2008) http://www.scribd.com/doc/92151/Attitude-is-everything

39 Canfield, Jack and Mark Victor Hansen. *Chicken Soup for the Soul*. Deerfield Beach, FL: Health Communications, Inc. 1993.

40 Peale, Norman Vincent. *The Power of Positive Thinking*. Upper Saddle River, New Jersey: Prentice Hall, Inc. 1952.

41 Milton, John. Paradise Regained a Poem in IV Books To which is added Samson Agonistes: The Second Book (lines 466–467). Renascence Editions: An Online Repository of Works Printed in English Between the Years 1477 and

1799, The University of Oregon 1992–2008. (Accessed November 27, 2008) http://darkwing.uoregon.edu/~rbear/regained.html .

42   Biographies Hall of Fame Nelson Rolihlahla Mandela. ZAR.com. January 2007. (Accessed January 10, 2008) http://zar.co.za/mandela.htm

43   Collier, Robert. *Secret of the Ages.* Radford, VA: Wilder Publications 2007.

44   Mandino, Og. *The Choice.* New York, NY: Bantam Books 1984.

45   Jerome, Jerry. *Instant Inspiration: Using Quotes to Guide You to Your Goals.* Phoenix, AZ: Instant Wisdom Publishing 2003.

46   Wholey, Dennis. *Are You Happy: Some Answers To The Most Important Question In Your Life.* Boston, MA: Houghton Mifflin 1986.

47   Hansen, Mark Victor and Robert G. Allen. *The One-Minute Millionaire: The Enlightened Way to Wealth.* New York, NY: Harmony Books 2002.

48   Tracy, Brian. *The Psychology of Achievement: Develop the Top Achiever's Mindset.* Niles, IL: Nightingale-Conant, Corp. 1994.

49   Ziglar, Zig. *Great Quotes from Zig Ziglar.* North Bergen, NJ: Book-mart Press 1997.

50   Burnham, Daniel H. Today in History: September 4. The Library of Congress American Memory 2008. (Accessed November 25, 2008) http://memory.loc.gov/ammem/today/sep04.html

51   Ameliaearhart.com. Quotes. Amelia Earhart The Official Website. (Accessed January 10, 2008) http://www.ameliaearhart.com/about/quotes.html

52   Beals, Gerald. Thomas Alva Edison: Be Enlightened. Thomas Edison.com February 11, 1997. (Accessed February 16, 2008) http://www.thomasedison.com/enlightened.html

53   Beals, Gerald. Thomas Alva Edison: Quotes. Thomas Edison.com February 11, 1997. (Accessed February 16, 2008) http://www.thomasedison.com/quotes.html

54   Tracy, Brian. *Successories Great Little Book on The Gift of Self Confidence.* North Bergen, NJ: Book-mart Press 1997.

55   Dyer, Wayne W. *Wisdom of the Ages: 60 Days to Enlightenment.* New York, NY: HarperCollins Publishers Inc. 1989.

56   Covey, Stephen R. *The 7 Habits of Highly Effective People,* New York, NY: Simon and Schuster 1989.

57   Murphy, Joseph. *Power of Your Subconscious Mind.* USA: Prentice Hall Trade 1963.

58   Proverbs 23:7, The King James Bible.

59   Bradford, Gertrude A. *The Subconscious Mind: How to Reach and Arouse.* Whitefish, MT: Kessinger Publishing, LLC 1942.

60   Proverbs 29:18, The King James Bible.

61   Hansen, Mark Victor and Robert G. Allen. *The One-Minute Millionaire: The Enlightened Way to Wealth.* New York, NY: Harmony Books 2002.

62   Hansen

63   Documentary

64   Hill, Napoleon. *Think and Grow Rich.* The Ralston Publishing Co. 1954.

65   Sagan, Carl. *The Cosmos.* New York, NY: Random House Publishing Group 1985.

66   Keefe, Simon P. *Mozart Studies.* Cambridge, UK: Cambridge University Press, 2006.

67   Einstein, Albert. *Cosmic Religion : With Other Opinions and Aphorisms.* New York, NY: Covici-Friede Publishing 1931.

68   Ray, James A. *The Science of Success: How to Attract Prosperity and Create Harmonic Wealth Through Proven Principles.* Carlsbad, CA: SunArk Press 2003.

69   Dyer, Wayne W. *Wisdom of the Ages: 60 Days to Enlightenment.* New York, NY: HarperCollins Publishers Inc. 1989.

70   *There's a Spiritual Solution to Every Problem.* Wayne W. Dyer. Public Broadcasting Service 2003.

71 There's a Spiritual Solution to Every Problem

72 *The Legend of Bagger Vance*. Dir. Robert Redford. Perf. Will Smith, Matt Damon, Charlize Theron, Bruce McGill, Joel Gretsch. DreamWorks, 2000. DVD. Dreamworks Video, April 3, 2001.

73 *The Legend of Bagger Vance*

74 Waitley, Denis. *Seeds of Greatness: The Ten Best-Kept Secrets of Total Success*. USA: Pocket 1988.

75 Meyer, Joyce. *100 Ways to Simplify Your Life*. New York, NY: Hachette Book Group 2007.

76 Hawkins, David R. *Power vs. Force*. Carlsbad, CA: Hay House Inc., 1995.

77 Shakespeare, William. Hamlet, Prince of Denmark. The Plays and Sonnets of William Shakespeare (Volume Two), Encyclopedia Britannica Great Books of the Western World. Edited by William George Clarke and William Aldis Wright. Chicago, IL: William Benton 1952.

78 Dyer, Wayne W. *Getting in the Gap: Making Conscious Contact with God Through Meditation*. Carlsbad, CA: Hay House, Inc. 2003.

79 Dyer

80 Dyer, Wayne W. *Everyday Wisdom for Success*. Carlsbad, CA: Hay House, Inc. 2006.

81 Morris, Tom. *Inner Discipline, Inner Power, Morris Institute Weekly Wisdom*. Morris Institute for Human Values 2008. (Accessed January 2008). http://www.morrisinstitute.com/index.php?s=wisdom&c=weekly_inner

82 Hill, Napoleon. *Think and Grow Rich*. The Ralston Publishing Co. 1954.

83 Hill

84 Napoleon Hill talks about his meeting with Andrew Carnegie. Napoleon Hill. YouTube 2008. (Accessed on November 24, 2008) http://www.youtube.com/watch?v=1GCaEZscfvA&feature=related

85 Napoleon Hill talks about his meeting with Andrew Carnegie.

86 Hill, Napoleon. *Think and Grow Rich.* New York, NY: Random House Publishing, Inc. 1960.

87 Hill

88 Hansen, Mark Victor and Robert G. Allen. *The One-Minute Millionaire: The Enlightened Way to Wealth.* New York, NY: Harmony Books 2002.

89 There's a Spiritual Solution to Every Problem. Dr. Wayne Dyer. Public Broadcasting Service 2003.

90 There's a Spiritual Solution to Every Problem

91 There's a Spiritual Solution to Every Problem

92 There's a Spiritual Solution to Every Problem

93 Allen, James. *The Wisdom of James Allen: Five Classic Works.* Ed. Zubko, Andy. San Diego, CA: Laurel Creek Press 1997.

94 Myers, Joyce. *The Power of Thoughts and Words, The Mind of Flesh, Managing Your Emotions.* Fenton, MO: Joyce Myers Ministries 2003, 1997, 2004.

95 Dyer, Wayne W. *Wisdom of the Ages: 60 Days to Enlightenment.* New York, NY: HarperCollins Publishers Inc. 1989.

96 Larson, Christian D. *Your Forces and How to Use Them (1912).* Whitefish, MT: Kessinger Publishing, LLC 2007.

97 Proverbs 13:2, The King James Bible.

98 Proverbs 18:21, The King James Bible.

99 Psalm 19:14, The King James Bible.

100 Hill, Napoleon. *Think and Grow Rich.* New York, NY: Random House Publishing, Inc. 1960.

101 Proverbs 10:21, The King James Bible.

102 Andersen, U.S. *Three Magic Words.* Chatsworth, CA: Wilshire Books Company 1980.

103 Ali.com. 2008. Muhammad Ali Enterprises LLC. (Accessed November 4, 2007) http://www.ali.com/index.aspx

104 Hill, Napoleon. *Think and Grow Rich.* New York, NY: Random House Publishing, Inc. 1960.

105 Dyer, Wayne W. *There's a Spiritual Solution to Every Problem.* New York, NY: HarperCollins Publishers Inc., 2003.

106 Jones, Susan Smith and Wayne W. Dyer. *Choose to be Healthy.* Berkley, CA: Celestial Arts 1987.

107 Proverbs 11:24. New American Standard Bible.

108 Walsch, Neale Donald. *Conversations with God: An Uncommon Dialogue (Book 1).* New York, NY: G.P. Putnam's Sons, 1996.

109 Walsch

110 Unlimited Power. Anthony Robbins. Nightingale Conant Corp. 1989

111 Tzu, Sun. *The Art of War.* U.S.A.: Filiquarian Publishing, LLC. 2006.

112 Altopp, David. *Coach Quotes for Baseball.* Monterey, CA: Coaches Choice 2000.

113 Dyer, Wayne W. *Living the Wisdom of the Tao, The Complete Tao Te Ching and Affirmations.* United States: Hay House, Inc., 2008.

114 Proverbs: 6:6–8, New American Standard Bible.

115 *NOVA: Little Creatures Who Run The World.* Perf. Bill Mason, Edward O. Wilson. WGBH-Boston: The Corporation for Public Broadcasting, August 12, 1997.

116 *NOVA: Little Creatures Who Run The World.*

117 Reese, Alice Anna and Carlynn Trout. Famous Missourians: James Cash Penney. The State Historical Society of Missouri 2008. (Accessed May 14, 2008) http://shs.umsystem.edu/famousmissourians/entrepreneurs/penney/penney.shtml#top

118 Reese

119 *Crazy Billionaire Speak: Motivational Quotes by Billionaires on Success, Business, and Life.* Hodderway Books 2008.

120 Scott, Steven K. *The Richest Man Who Ever Lived: King Solomon's Secrets to Success, Wealth, and Happiness.* New York, NY: Broadway Books 2006.

121 Ecclesiastes 4:9, New King James Bible.

122 Proverbs 11:14, New King James Bible.

123 Ibid

124 Proverbs 15:22, New American Standard Bible.

125 Roosevelt, Theodore. Citizenship in a Republic *(Speech).* Sorbonne, Paris, France, 1910.

126 Rumi, Jalal al-Din Muhammad. Epitaph (Inscribed upon Rumi's Tomb).

127 Hill, Napoleon. *Think and Grow Rich.* New York, NY: Random House Publishing, Inc. 1960.

128 MacIver, Roderick. *Thoreau and the Art of Life: Precepts and Principles.* North Ferrisburg, VT: Heron Dance Press and Art Studio 2006.

129 Matthew 25:21, The King James Bible.

130 Schucman, Helen. *A Course in Miracles.* Mill Valley, CA: The Foundation for Inner Peace 1976.

131 Hebrews 11:3, New International Bible.

132 Daniels, Peter J. Living on the Edge: The Autobiography of Peter J. Daniels. World Centre for Entrepreneurial Studies 2003.

133 Tolle, Eckhart. *The Power of Now: A Guide to Spiritual Enlightenment.* Novato, CA: New World Library 1999. Vancouver b.c., Canada: Namaste Publishing 1999.

134 Jerome, Jerry. *Instant Inspiration: Using Quotes to Guide You to Your Goals.* Phoenix, AZ: Instant Wisdom Publishing 2003.

135 Shaw, George Bernard. *Man and Superman: A Comedy and a Philosophy.* Cambridge, U.S.A: The University Press 1903.

136 Daniels, Peter J. Living on the Edge: The Autobiography of Peter J. Daniels. World Centre for Entrepreneurial Studies 2003.

137 Williamson, Marianne. *A Return to Love: Reflections on the Principles of A Course in Miracles.* New York, NY: Harper Collins 1992.

138 *The Eleventh Hour.* Dir. Nadia Connors, Leila Connors Petersen. Perf. Leonardo DiCaprio, Thom Hartmann. Warner Home Video, 2008.

139 *The Eleventh Hour*

140 Wilcox, Ella Wheeler. Poems of Ella Wheeler Wilcox. Charleston, SC: BiblioBazaar 2007.

141 The Oprah Winfrey Show: Women Across the Globe. Perf. Oprah Winfrey. HARPO Studios, May 2005.

142 The Oprah Winfrey Show: Women Across the Globe.

143 The Oprah Winfrey Show: Women Across the Globe.

144 Human Development Indices: A statistical update 2008 - HDI rankings. United Nations Development Programme (UNDP.org). (Accessed December 22, 2008) *|FCO|Hyperlinkhttp://hdr.undp.org/en/statistics/.|FCC|*

145 Carlin, John. "No wonder Iceland has the happiest people on earth." *The Observer*, May 18, 2008. (Accessed December 22, 2008) http://www.guardian. co.uk/world/2008/may/18/iceland .

146 Carlin

147 Carlin

148 Carlin

149 Carlin

150 Hansen, Mark Victor and Robert G. Allen. *The One-Minute Millionaire: The Enlightened Way to Wealth.* New York, NY: Harmony Books 2002.

151 Walsch, Neale Donald. *Conversations with God: An Uncommon Dialogue (Book 1).* New York, NY: G.P. Putnam's Sons, 1996.

listen|imagine|view|experience

AUDIO BOOK DOWNLOAD INCLUDED WITH THIS BOOK!

In your hands you hold a complete digital entertainment package. In addition to the paper version, you receive a free download of the audio version of this book. Simply use the code listed below when visiting our website. Once downloaded to your computer, you can listen to the book through your computer's speakers, burn it to an audio CD or save the file to your portable music device (such as Apple's popular iPod) and listen on the go!

How to get your free audio book digital download:

1. Visit www.tatepublishing.com and click on the e|LIVE logo on the home page.
2. Enter the following coupon code:
   d619-e864-9e57-3c88-aaf9-3df8-7090-d54a
3. Download the audio book from your e|LIVE digital locker and begin enjoying your new digital entertainment package today!